DIGITAL STRATEGIES 4 MUSIC INDUSTRY SUCCESS

© Joyce Logan, 2018

I dedicate this book to mama who believed in me and to the entire music industry which is the inspiration for this book. I saw what happened over the past two decades as recording companies fell off the map and new and seasoned artists had nowhere to go to nurture and successfully expose their talent. I made it my business to find the fix. It was a long tedious process, but I did it.

Table of Contents

INTRODUCTION 1

CHAPTER ONE – THE RESEARCH 3

    The Research Sparked It All..3

    Marketing - Old School Success..6

    Ups and Downs in the Music Industry 7

    Digital Skills are Still Lacking 8

    The Study Participants 10

    A Definition of Terms used in the Study: 10

    How the Study Was Conducted 11

    What the Research Revealed 12

    Findings 17

    Summary...18

    Findings and Conclusion 19

    Recommendations for Future Research..22

CHAPTER TWO – HISTORY 101..25

    Historical Challenges and Victories in the Music Industry 25

    The Phonograph Changed the Music Industry 25

    The Big Three: Edison-Victor-Columbia Records 26

    RCA Victor is Born 27

    The Jukebox Challenges the Industry..27

    The AFM Strike for Pay 28

    Changing Methods of Music Delivery 29

    Payola 30

    MTV 30

    The CD Craze 30

    Napster: The Predecessor to Music Piracy 31

    Progression of the Digital Age 32

    Maintaining the Legacy of Recorded Sound 32

    Artists, Musicians, and Production 33

    Internet Music Sales 34

    CD Baby 34

    Social Media Explosion 34

    Social Media Platform 35

    Social Media and the Executive Leader 36

    Music Streaming 36

    Summary 38

CHAPTER THREE – SKILLS & STRATEGIES 40

    First things first 40

    Radio 40

    Social Media Marketing - Strategy 41

    Social Media Analytics and Management 44

    The website - Strategy 44

    Search Engine Optimization (SEO) - Strategy 45

    Marketing Analytics 47

Driving the Car	48
ABOUT THE AUTHOR	49
THE RESEARCH - REFERENCES	54
MY SUCCESS STEPS AND JOURNAL	72

INTRODUCTION

Technology changed the entire make-up of the music industry. I can't say it took everyone by surprise because it didn't take place overnight but over a period of time. The goal of this book is to reveal where music industry personnel currently stand regarding new technology and digital strategies; briefly chronicle how new technology affected the music industry over decades; how technology used strategically can propel companies and artists towards success in the music industry. The book will provide marketing insight and resources that will allow industry leaders, artists, and personnel to become more skillful and successful in the music business utilizing digital skills, strategies and techniques. Leaders in the recorded music industry have been uncertain as to what digital resources and strategies are essential to managing the collapse in the industry since the beginning of the digital music revolution. I conducted a three-year study that explored the digital skills and strategies needed to lead a successful recorded music organization. The study was conducted from the standpoint of executive leaders and not my own assumptions. History of the music industry, encompassing the forms of digital media and the need and strength of social media, innovations, and technology sets the backdrop for this book. In-depth interviews were conducted, recorded and transcribed. Detailed analysis of the responses showed that communication remains the key factor in all the participants' success in the music industry, but there remains a need for greater knowledge and training in digital skills and strategies. The study concluded that when leaders at recorded music organizations utilize ongoing research and application in the areas of Search engine optimization (SEO), social media marketing, digital promotion, distribution, and branding to further develop their needed digital strategies, their businesses and careers can better compete in the market. With added knowledge and utilization of resources leaders can perform more efficiently in the market and by utilizing tools that provide live streaming, leaders can gain a significant amount of the market share. The recommendation further included online training in digital marketing, promotion, and branding.

CHAPTER ONE – THE RESEARCH

The Research Sparked It All

Ten years ago, I would never have imagined writing this book. I would never have imagined receiving a doctorate degree that became the incentive to this book. For years I had always asked, " how can I be a benefit to others and yet live? When I started the doctorate program I thought my dissertation was going to be primarily on leadership because of my doctoral concentration – Executive Leadership. Therefore, I proceeded to gather pertinent information and do research around management and executive leadership. I gleaned much from the world's definition of leadership from corporate perspectives. But I was determined to maintain balance in my life as a Christian woman. I'd seen peers enter universities as strong Christians and come out as watered down purely academic spewing citizens and the "fire" they once displayed on the spiritual side seemed watered down or gone. I did not want that to happen to me. So, in addition to my academic and scholarly studies I researched and explored leadership from well-known clergy and speakers such as John Maxwell, T.D Jakes, Augustine of Hippo, and Benjamin Carson to name a few, to keep balance in my life while studying the topic.

The dissertation was coming along just fine, but the document was laced with lots of technological jargon because of my passion for technology. My professors each encouraged and suggested I take another route with my writing while keeping the theme of leadership in it. They knew of my musical background and my technical skills, knowledge, and notoriety in the field of technology as it pertained to the music industry. They were aware of my success as a publisher of a national trade magazine and online video magazine. It was the university's suggestion that I enter the degree program that I selected. It was never a desire of mine to go back to college let alone choose Management with a concentration on Executive Leadership. After all, hadn't I already proved that I was leadership capable? But Gods orchestration is awesome when we don't even have a clue what he's doing in our lives most times.

Although it is common while working on a doctorate degree, not to have the final dissertation title until after the second year into the program, my title took a new route. One of my professors suggested a possible title that I fell in love with, and the new title then became: Exploring the Digital Skills Needed to Lead a Successful Music Recording Organization. As time passed I realized I did not want to limit myself to just recording companies but to any person or organization who created, marketed, or played the music. I didn't want to limit the study to simply skills. My dissertation title then evolved six months before I graduated to become The Digital Strategies Needed to Lead a Successful Recorded Music Organization. By broadening the study's title, I broadened the research and the scope of the document and thusly the book title –Digital Strategies for Music Industry Success.

What a joy it was for me to research that topic. It was right down my alley. The professors all found it to be a very enlightening and informative work and pushed me hard. The demands on me were rigid and challenging as they could see in my dissertation a book emerging that would help thousands of who had lost their way within the industry or just didn't know where to start amid all the technical jargon.

I painstakingly earned the title Dr. Joyce Logan, DM-Executive Leadership. I did the research. I interviewed the executives. I put the marketing plans into place and now I can share it with the world. The dissertation was too academically and scholarly written for the general public to enjoy reading and would in my opinion have been to mundane and boring for creative minds. So, the language has been edited and changed to the journalistic style of Joyce Logan while maintaining the full message of the manuscript. I want the book to be fun to read and I want you to have a hard time putting it down as you read thru the pages. The first chapters outline my three-year study. The remainder of the book features information that will hopefully take your business or career the next level of digital success.

Knowing the ins and outs of the record business is a plus when it comes to digitizing marketing, promotion, and distribution. I envisioned and launched a highly successful publishing business for many years using the same skills and know how. But more than anything I've remained on top of cutting edge technology as it continues to evolve at breakneck speed. The music industry is a totally new bird now and musicians, artists, promoters, managers, etc. have nowhere to go except up - digitally. Long gone are the days of sales reps visiting key record shops and dropping by the local radio stations with new product as the primary means of marketing and promoting the product. I found in my three-year study that today many still don't know what resources are available, or what skills to use. This book is designed to bridge that gap.

It does not matter what the culture is of those seeking help and guidance in their business and or careers. It does not matter what the genre of music is. All within the music industry were gravely affected by the wave of technology that swept thru and wiped many music industry VIP's off the music industry landscape. Therefore, this book is not music genre specific but relative to anyone needing the digital skills and strategies to be successful in any business.

I felt it necessary to share brief historical moments that present not only the history of the music industry but challenges and changes that occurred over time as the industry developed. Many believe that new technology changed the face of the industry for the first time since the beginning of music as a business, but my study shows that there were many major challenges and changes that took place prior to the invasion of technology. Each challenge posed what appeared to be a grave future for the music industry, yet each brought about a great change. If you read no more of the book after reading the history, you will know much more about the evolution of recorded music than the average person. My goal is to help you create your very own success story and pay it forward.

Marketing - Old School Success

Recording companies understood that to have a successful project on their hands there had to be a series of tasks performed prior to the release of the project to ensure the success of the project. The tasks didn't start and stop with publishing rights and a great recording but included letting radio and retail know that the project was about to "drop". It included "coming soon" announcements in trade publications and key media outlets. The tasks included great packaging of the project. Companies understood the importance of product packaging that featured more than just a photo of the artist or group, but told a story in the graphics and design of the cover. Would a person pick the product off the shelf and consider buying it without first hearing it based on the cover art? This was an important consideration taken in presenting a visual quality product to the market place. Then there were the sales teams who were responsible for certain regions of the state and country. These sales reps were given the responsibility of physically taking upcoming release samples or newly released product into key radio and retail outlets in their assigned regions and then tracking that product (physically calling individual stations, daily and weekly) to see if the product was being played and how often the rotation of play was. Sales were tracked to see if and how the product was selling in their regions. Because of consistent tracking of radio and retail, the recording company was able to get firsthand information about the ongoing life of the released product. Who knew then that all of this would one day be performed digitally?

In many cases high visibility of an artist's product at radio and retail ensured that the artist or group got into major performance venues. Marketing and promoting the artist was and still is primarily handled by artist management, an agency, or publicist, although individuals can literally market and promote their own product using today's technology methods. Bookings and tour dates were secured and confirmed. Radio and retail ads were purchased and tracked by management often in partnership with the record label. Venue ticket sales were tracked, etc. The consistency and professionalism of all these efforts led to high volume sales and bookings for artists. In many cases managers, agencies, publicists, radio, retail and the recording company worked together as a team to ensure the success of the project. All of this was done at a time when digital technology was unheard of or in the infant stages of development. These efforts and more led to a successful recorded music organization.

Ups and Downs in the Music Industry

Digital skills and strategies have become increasingly important in every aspect of the business world and particularly the music industry, especially for managers working in executive leadership roles. Digital strategies have a major effect on the continued success of the music industry. As technology advances at alarming speed, music industry personnel have many important responsibilities, including the ongoing research and development of digital skills and strategies.

A leader, be it a recording company executive, artist, management, publicist, or promoter, must have an objective outlook regarding what is going on within the company or his or her career, what technological advances are shaping the marketplace, and how those changes impact the success of the organization or individual career. Some who are out of touch with the strategies required to be successful in a modern organization have offered contradictory views regarding digital knowledge.

Organizations often struggle to survive when their strategies are deficient. By understanding what strategies are needed, it may be possible to determine what technologies are necessary. Success in the recorded music industry has become dependent upon whether leaders can adjust to the changing technological environment of the music industry.

Well established digital skills and strategies are vital to the success of the music industry. Those who take advantage of new technology may gain a better understanding of demographics that are vital to music distribution and the marketing techniques required to reach these demographics. Without advanced digital skills and strategies, recorded music organizations will continue to lose their competitive edge in the music industry and literally become extinct.

The development and maintenance of digital skills and strategies is essential to the growth and survival of the recorded music industry. Music personnel must therefore display the innovative mindset needed to accomplish the goals of their company or individual career. By defining the digital skills and strategies that are necessary, a company may develop a plan to move towards a prosperous outcome.

Digital Skills are Still Lacking

Over the past 2 decades, researchers have noted that digital strategies are lacking in the recorded music industry. While some record labels have improved their performance and management, many facets of the sector have not achieved the same level of expectation. This lack of digital strategies and skills has created a shortage of recorded music organizations.

Reviewing past and current research revealed a need for music industry personnel to embrace change and become more advanced in digital skills and strategies. Within the music industry, however, this problem remains unsolved. Scholars have shown that for the music industry to become stronger, executive leadership and music industry personnel must embrace and employ advanced digital skills and strategies in the areas of music creation, demographics, marketing, and distribution. These strategies will enable leaders to (a) study demographics, (b) embrace and utilize technology tools, (c) use online music distribution sources, and (d) utilize online marketing tools. These digital strategies are a critical factor in the successful leadership of a recorded music organization.

The problem addressed in this study was that the digital music revolution revealed uncertainty regarding which digital strategies would best promote the growth of music recording organizations. The success of these organizations is often dependent upon whether their leaders can adapt to the evolving technological environment within the recorded music industry. Having reviewed the external reasons for the music industry collapse—such as piracy and free downloading of music product— internal digital strategies were explored.

Mastering digital strategies requires the ability to successfully navigate, gauge, and generate information using an array of digital technologies to achieve important aims. Being digitally literate is an ongoing process in which individuals must consistently and actively try new technology tools and resources, build strategies with these techniques, and use these technologies to meet their needs and achieve their goals. When individuals consistently keep up with technology, learn new digital resources, and effectively use these skills, they are exercising the ongoing process of digital mastery.

In this study, I discovered that there was an underlying assumption that the recorded music industry had suffered significant changes and collapsed due to the deficit in digital strategies by executive leaders. In conducting the three-year study, the assumption was that the sample participants who were chosen to respond to the questions would have insights into the primary question, "What digital strategies are needed to successfully lead a recording music organization? I had a significant awareness of the topic, having worked as an executive leader in the music industry for over 40 years. In the past, as new technologies entered the market, I utilized new techniques and was successful with the outcomes received. In addition, I was a beta tester for the introduction of Facebook and other interactive technologies. These experiences did not affect my judgment or performance as an ethical and unbiased investigator during this study. I set aside my personal feelings and any presumptions of existing problems and issues to objectively analyze the data collected during the study.

The study was unique because the investigation was conducted during a time when strategy needs were rapidly changing to accommodate the evolving music industry, and that remains true today. The significance of the study revealed that music industry personnel needed to stay abreast of technological changes that directly and/or indirectly affect their ability to lead a successful recorded music organization.

The Study Participants

A sampling of the music industry population included successful music industry personnel in the recorded music industry who were interviewed. During the interview, focus was not centered on the causes for the collapse of the industry; rather, the questions concentrated on the digital strategies needed to lead a successful recorded music organization. Following is a definition of terms used in the book.

A Definition of Terms used in the Study:

Executive leader. An executive leader provides organizational goals, decision-making, and strategic planning in an organization, while guiding and influencing others in the organization.

Music industry. The music industry is an economic profession consisting of composers, songwriters, vocalists, musicians, companies, and professionals who create, play, market, and sell recorded music.

Music piracy. Music piracy refers to the process of copying and distributing music without the permission of the artist, composer, or company holding the copyright.

Music recording organization. A music recording organization is a record label or music publishing company. The company seeks new talent and develops the artist and coordinates the production of music. The company also manufactures and distributes the music.

Recorded music organization. This term includes music management companies, promotional firms, radio stations, music advertising companies, and musical groups.

The information collected from each research participant was not based on numbers, calculations, or demographics, but rather performed an informal grouping of music industry and digital technology topics and questions asked in different ways for different participants during interviews, resulting in realistic and illustrative information. The study was designed to collect factual and current information concerning the digital skills and strategies of music industry leaders.

How the Study Was Conducted

A qualitative exploratory approach was used to guide this study by securing interview data from leaders who were or had been successful in creating high visibility for their music recording organization. The research participants were recruited from recorded music organizations located in various cities around the country.

The recorded information was transcribed and coded using analytical software. The general approach of the data analysis included compiling the interview data, organizing each participant's interview, recognizing the categories by coding the data, classifying themes, and establishing relationships by identifying differences and similarities in the themes. The themed categories became the conclusions of the study and derived patterns and themes from the data to develop a thematic framework for the study.

What the Research Revealed

The importance of digital strategies is to maintain an objective outlook on what is going on within the company and the marketplace and the rate of interest (ROI). There is a significant relationship between ability to adjust to advances in technology and the success of an organization. Digital strategies are often complicated and drawn out, however, by conflicting views. The study was created as an exploration of the strategies that music industry managers need to lead a successful music recording organization.

Three primary themes resulted from the interview data. "Communication" was the central theme throughout the analysis of data, and "Need More Digital Training", followed by "Keeping the Artist Visible" and "Maintaining Branding".

The first interview question asked, "As a successful leader in the music industry, to what do you attribute your success?" Based on the response of the participants, 90% of the participants indicated that effective communication was key to their success, indicating the music industry is a people industry. The remaining 10% expressed that technology was key to their success.

The second interview question asked, "What digital strategies did you or are you using to achieve success as a leader?" Eighty percent of the participants expressed that communication was a key factor in their success but did not express usage of digital strategies; the remaining 20% expressed technology as key to their success and listed strategies used.

The third interview question asked, "What are your thoughts about new technology in the music industry?" Sixty percent of the participants indicated that technology was critical or important to the industry but that it was still too complicated; 10% expressed communication as an ongoing need for success and how technology had increased communication with both artists and consumers; 30% revealed a need for more digital training but did not know where to start as it related to technology.

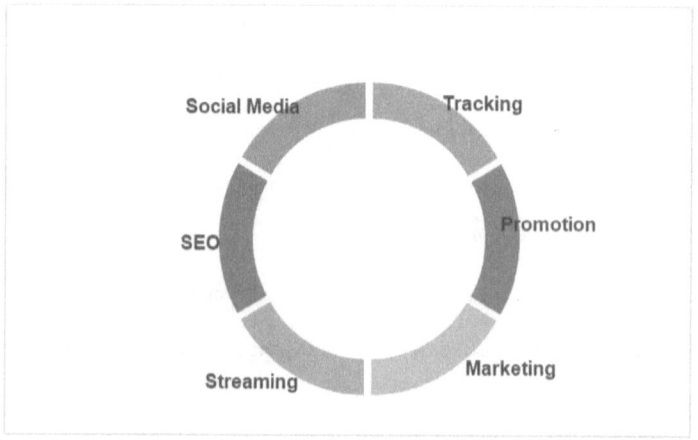

Keeping the Artist Visible and Maintaining Branding theme. Digital strategies encompass social media, tracking, SEO, marketing, streaming, and promotion.

The fourth interview question asked, "What methods or tools regarding technology are you familiar?" The primary theme developed from the responses to this question was Keeping the Artist Visible and Maintaining Branding. All the participants responded that they were familiar with digital tools. Thirty-nine percent of the participants were familiar with and used Facebook, 18% were familiar with Twitter, 17% were familiar with Instagram, 13% were familiar with YouTube, 9% were familiar with Snapchat, and 4% were familiar with iTunes

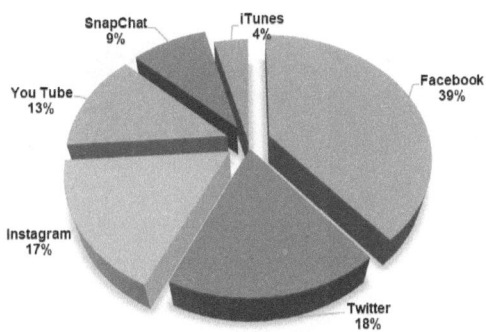

Most familiar digital tools for strategies by participants and percentages of responses

The fifth interview question asked, "What are the most important digital technology strategies that you currently use?". Although all participants were familiar with digital tools, only 45% used Facebook, 10% used Twitter, 10% used Instagram, and 15% used YouTube in their music industry business.

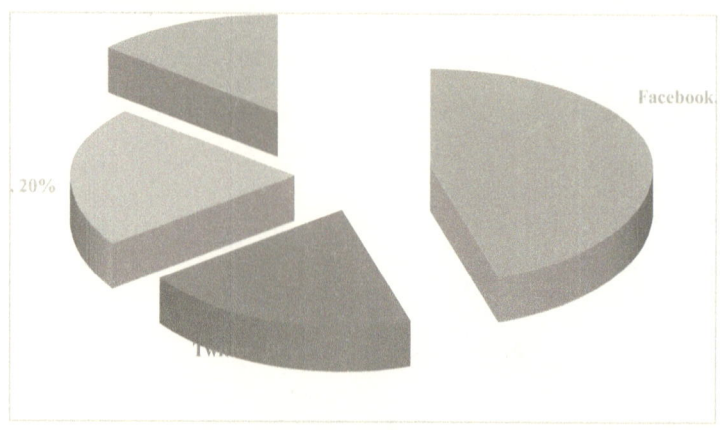

Top four digital tools for strategy most used by participants and percentages of responses.

The sixth interview question asked, "What are the least important digital strategies that you currently use?" Of the digital strategies least used, Twitter stood out, with 50% of responses revealing that the strategy is least used; 10% used Snapchat very little, 10% least used Facebook, 10% least used Instagram, and 10% least used email. As of this book release the use of Twitter has increased by 20%

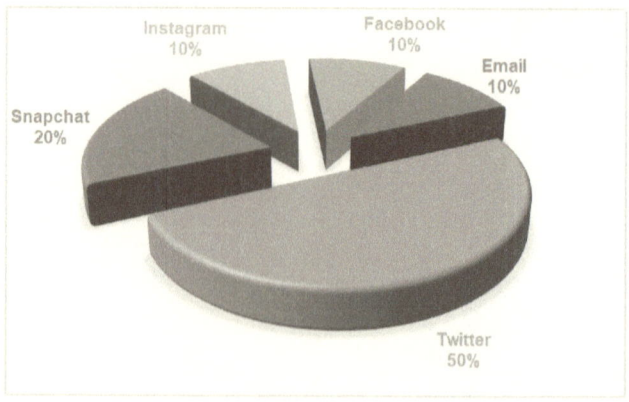

Digital tools for strategy least used by participants and percentages of responses.

The seventh interview question asked, "What digital strategies that you currently use needs to be improved?" Forty percent of the participants responded with needing improvement in Twitter, 10% responded with needing improvement in YouTube, 10% responded with needing improvement in live streaming, 10% responded with needing improvement in HootSuite, and 10% responded with needing improvement in Instagram.

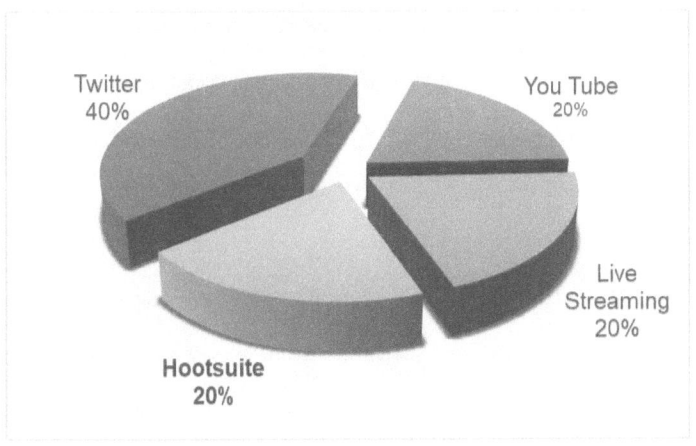

Participants desire improvement in using these tools for strategy and percentages of responses.

The eighth research question asked, "What digital strategies that you currently use would you like to change?" Of the 10 participants wanting to change their performance in digital tools for strategies, 30% wanted to change or improve their performance in Facebook, 20% wanted to change their performance in tracking royalties, 10% of participants wanted to change and improve their performance in live streaming, and 10% wished to change their performance in Twitter.

The ninth interview question asked, "Are there any digital strategies that you would like to have more training?" Forty percent of the participants indicated a desire for more training with live streaming, 20% responded with Twitter, 20% responded with Facebook, 10% responded with digital marketing, 10% responded with digital branding, and 10% responded with Hootsuite

The tenth interview question asked, "What digital skills and strategies are needed in your opinion, to successfully sustain the music industry?" Eighty percent of the participants indicated that communication was a necessary leadership skill and communication strategies were critical, 10% responded that strategies with technology were needed, and 10% indicated that they need more digital training to be able to compete in the market.

Findings

The findings revealed that music industry personnel were consistent in their responses that communication using digital skills and strategies remains the key factor in their success as a leader within the industry. When asked the question, "As a successful leader in the music industry, to what do you attribute your success?" One participant stated, "Staying abreast of what the people need and want in the marketplace. I listen to the people. I try very hard to stay on top of the latest trends and resources that will help me to improve my performance in the business and in myself." The findings further showed that each participant recognized how technology affected and changed the music industry and their prior performance and strategy sets in the industry. Each participant revealed that Facebook was their primary digital tool for strategy used but that they needed and wanted more training in other digital tools for strategies such as Twitter, Instagram, YouTube, and HootSuite. Live streaming of recorded product was a concern of a small percentage of the executive leaders. The participants' responses supported the thought that although music industry personnel do utilize some digital strategies, there is a need for greater training and usage of other digital strategies to remain competitive in the industry. In response to the question, "Are there any digital strategies that you would like to have more training?" one of the participants stated, "I would maybe like to know more about how streaming works because I know now that it counts toward sales. I don't have a lot of knowledge in that area."

Summary

The study indicated an understanding from the standpoint of music industry personnel what digital strategies were most and least used. The results of the data analysis revealed three themes: (a) Communication, (b) Need More Digital Training, and (c) Keeping the Artist Visible and Maintaining Branding. A subtheme of each was a Lack of Digital Strategies Initiatives. The findings showed that communication using digital strategies was and remains the key factor in each participant's success, but that lack of digital strategies initiatives caused changes in the music industry. The findings revealed that keeping the artist visible and maintaining branding was and remains the key element to their success as a leader within the industry. Findings showed that each participant recognized how technology affected and changed their performance and strategy sets in the industry. The results of the study revealed that Facebook is the primary digital tool used, but that more training in other digital tools for strategies is desired and needed to provide adequate digital strategies.

By knowing the strategies required, it would be possible to uncover what technology is necessary to lead a successful recorded music organization. Researchers have indicated that critical digital strategies in the recorded music industry are dependent upon whether leaders are able to adapt to the changing technological environment of the industry.

Being digitally literate is an ongoing process in which individuals consistently and actively learn technology tools and resources, build strategies with new techniques, and use technologies to meet their needs and achieve their goals. When individuals are consistent in keeping up with technology, digital resources, and digital strategies, they are exercising the ongoing process of digital literacy.

Digital strategies have become increasingly important in the recorded music industry especially for managers working in executive leadership roles. These strategies have a significant effect in ensuring the continued success of the industry.

Findings and Conclusion

The initial question asked of each participant was, "As a successful leader in the music industry, what do you attribute your success to?" Each participant was eager to share what they attributed their success to and why. Each was asked to define their feelings and opinions about new technology and how the music industry was affected. All participants shared their position as executives and managers concerning the digital skills and strategies needed to improve and benefit their company, as well as the digital skills and strategies in which they would like to have more training.

The participants' responses supported the initial problem statement of the research that these organizational leaders were unsure what digital strategies were key to handling the instability in their industry. The themes, subtheme, and specific experiences shared by the participants revealed that they are unsure of and deficient in digital strategies but are eager and willing to acquire the strategies that are necessary for success in the industry.

The participants overwhelmingly revealed that a communicative relationship with artists and fans was vital in sustaining the industry and was the factor that in the past attributed to their success. Success depends greatly on the ability to work as a group or team—whether in decision-making, solving problems, or exchanging information. All participants responded that communication is a primary skill required to sustain the music industry, and that digital strategies require technological tools designed to communicate.

Although the participants desired training in digital strategies that were productive in communication practices such as Facebook and Twitter, participants expressed that digital marketing, promotion, and tracking tools were also a desired need. For most participants, the digital tools for strategy that they used most frequently was the social media tool, Facebook. With a limited understanding of Facebook's total resources and capabilities for expansion, the participants were unsure of the potential reach that Facebook provided. Communication was still the outstanding variable in all responses. Participants shared their concerns regarding the live streaming of music products and expressed that they felt intimidated by the need to better understand and utilize live streaming digital resource tools. Streaming is a technology tool that delivers audio and video content over the Internet in real time, meaning that recipients can listen immediately to the continuous flow of transmitted data. However, participants did not understand how to effectively generate revenue from live streaming sources. Another skill that participants shared a lack of understanding of—but had the desired need for training in—was HootSuite, a software tool that manages multiple social networks while connecting with clients and growing the company's brand on social media. A direct connection to the consumer is via social media marketing.

The participants felt that technology had definitively affected the music industry. The participants described how technology had made it so they could more effectively communicate with their artists and with the public. Each participant recognized how technology had affected and changed their performance and skills sets related to artist visibility and organizational branding. The results revealed the percentages of digital tools understood and used but not employed by the study participants. The results of the analyzed data further substantiated the underlying problem that these organizational leaders are unsure of what technological strategies are required to keep the artist visible and maintain branding.

The participants overwhelmingly revealed that a communicative relationship with artists and fans was vital in sustaining the industry and was the factor that in the past attributed to their success. The findings revealed that communication with the artists and the public was and remains the key element to their success as a leader within the industry. Success depends greatly on the ability to work as a group or team—whether in decision-making, solving problems, or exchanging information. All participants responded that communication is a primary strategy required to sustain the music industry, and that digital strategies are technological tools designed to communicate in a people industry.

Although the participants desired training in digital strategies that were productive in communication practices such as Facebook and Twitter, participants expressed that digital marketing, promotion, and tracking tools were also a desired need. For most participants, the digital strategy that they used most frequently was the social media tool, Facebook. With a limited understanding of Facebook's total resources and capabilities for expansion, the participants were unsure of the potential reach that Facebook provided. digital strategies were still the outstanding variable in all responses, of which a lack of digital strategies initiatives was the underlying subtheme. Participants shared their concerns regarding the live streaming of music products and expressed that they felt intimidated by the need to better understand and utilize live streaming digital resource tools. Based on the response to questions 1, 2, and, 10 none of the participants responded with strategic digital initiatives to achieve success. Only one of the participants responded with employing people from different areas of the organization working together as a team to deliver a consistent digital customer experience. The collective responses showed a lack of digital strategy initiatives.

The results of this study were dependent on the honesty of the participants and confined to the integrity of the participants during the interviews. The study was limited by time allotted for each meeting. This study was limited to the lived experiences of the participants within the music industry and was restricted by the demographics of the selected research participants.

Current findings were compared to those reviewed earlier. Noted were the similarities in the setbacks and challenges experienced by the music industry over time and those in other changing fields. When we look at history, in all cases, communication in a people industry was essential and the technology of the day was always the catalyst for the changes that took place within the industry.

With each change came a more improved method of delivery or visibility. Although music industry personnel at recorded music companies initially suffered great losses, they too had incredible options for survival within the industry. In today's music industry climate, survival entails greater digital strategies needed by executive leaders. As some music industry personnel choose to embrace new technology, their companies can once again enjoy the successes of the past. A good example of such adaption is how artists and record labels receive traditional royalties via online tracking and distribution of funds using a streaming service such as Pandora, Spotify, or Sirius Internet Radio. Another example is these companies' utilization of Search Engine Optimization (SEO) technology to create greater visibility for the company and the artists.

Recommendations for Future Research

The participants of this study expressed a need for more digital strategies training from communication to marketing to production. Communication was a primary response when asked how to maintain success. As technology sources continue to advance at a breakneck pace, what seems apparent from the responses generated during the study is that leaders must constantly stay abreast of newly developing technology. The results of this study revealed a necessity for incorporation of mandatory digital strategies training. Hiring employees with these required strategies and skills is critical to the continued success of the music organizations. The collective responses showed a lack of digital strategy initiatives. Recommendations are that recorded music organizations define their ultimate goals, secure needed digital training, and utilize the necessary digital strategies that afford them the desired success of those aims. Resources and expertise in social media are vital, as is digital marketing and promotion, tracking resources, and digital strategies tailored to deliver and increase visibility and branding. A further recommendation is the ongoing conduction of research as technology continues to evolve. Recommendations are that music industry personnel and management fully embrace technology and not be intimidated by it. With added resources and strategic initiatives such as live video syndication and the notification for higher visibility of artists, leaders can perform more efficiently in the market. By utilizing tools that provide live streaming, enabling the user to broadcast live at any time and from anywhere to anyone, leaders can gain a significant amount of the market share. The researcher's recommendations for practice would also include online training in digital tools, resources, and strategies, to include social media management, marketing analysis, digital promotion, and online branding.

Conclusion

Over the past 2 decades, there has been a deficiency of digital leadership skills in the recorded music industry. While some record labels have improved their digital performance and management, there are facets of the sector that have not achieved the same level of expectation. Researchers have indicated that leaders in the recorded music industry generally lack digital strategies. This lack of digital strategy has created a shortage of recorded music organizations; thus, there is a need to circumvent the added loss of executive leadership at recorded music organizations.

The purpose of this study was to understand what digital strategies are valuable in leading a successful recorded music organization from the standpoint of music industry personnel in the music industry. The results of the study revealed a scarcity of digital strategies that may have affected the downsizing of the recorded music industry. The significance of the study showed the importance of music industry personnel staying abreast of technological advances that directly and or indirectly affect the ability to lead a successful recorded music organization.

The data analysis revealed three primary themes and one subtheme. The three themes were: Communication, Need More Digital Training, followed by Keeping the Artist Visible and Maintaining Branding. The subtheme was Lack of Digital Strategies Initiatives. The findings showed that communication with the artists and the public was and remains the key factor in the success of a leader within the industry. The second theme indicated the fact that although management and leadership were familiar with digital strategies and resources, they did not adequately include this skill set in their business. Most participants expressed a need for more training, as well as the belief that it would help them to become more successful in their goal of greater communication. Participants felt that technology had definitively affected and changed the music industry and how to keep the artist visible and maintain branding. The participants concurred that technology had transformed the way they could more effectively communicate with their artists and with the public but that there remains a lack of digital strategies initiatives. The results of this research may act as a catalyst towards promoting increased motivation in leadership, increasing training, and utilizing greater digital strategies, leading to success in recorded music organizations.

CHAPTER TWO – HISTORY 101

Historical Challenges and Victories in the Music Industry

Strategies and techniques have flourished in the music industry since the 1800s. The music industry has undergone many challenges since this time, from the invention of the phonograph to digital music downloads to live streaming. With each new technology came accompanying turmoil and uncertainty within the industry. This chapter reviews a segment of music industry history to illustrate that for over 100 years, there has always been a wave of new technology that has brought concern and changes to the industry. The challenge today, however, is that faster and more advanced technological innovations affect the music industry at increasing rates. This chapter explores the challenges and changes that took place in past seasons of the music industry and what strategies led to successful change.

The Phonograph Changed the Music Industry

In the 1890s, the phonograph was still new. Although the reproduction of music is dated back as far as 1500 BC, documented experiments date back to the early 1800s and the phonograph. The only recorded evidence of another phonograph is from a French scientist, Charles Cross. Cross never brought forth the physical product, and his invention remained as a theory only; therefore, he was never given credit, as Thomas Edison ultimately produced a physical product. Edison's intent was not to perfect the phonograph but was compelled to do so because of the increasing competition from others to make the device commercially marketable.

Cross created a recording disk that gave birth to the music industry. Edison sent delegates, equipment, and cylinders to Europe almost as soon as he had invented the phonograph. From 1888 to 1894, recordings were made by such notables as Alfred Lord Tennyson, Johannes Brahms, and Robert Browning, although the first to record was 12-year-old Josef Hofmann in 1888.

Improving upon Edison's invention of the phonograph and the disc created by Cross was an American born in Germany, Emile Berliner, whose digital recording strategy moved him towards inventing the gramophone. Berliner further developed the record player or phonograph, which reproduced sound by using a stylus in the grooves of the flat disc. Between 1888 and 1894, recorded voice and musical compositions became popular. Previously, listening to music required either attending live concerts or purchasing the printed music and lyrics; now, people could listen to others' musical compositions on a record player.

New technology and a standard of listening to music allowed recording artists to gain fame and receive payment for their recorded music. Exposure became available for artists and budding recording labels. The first such company was the Edison Speaking Phonograph Company. In 1888, a major competitor for Edison was Columbia Phonograph Company, who also developed phonographs for the home.

The Big Three: Edison-Victor-Columbia Records

In Camden, New Jersey in 1901, Eldridge Johnson and Emile Berliner founded Victor Talking Machine Company, a record label that also manufactured phonographs that did not need hand cranks. In 1902, the company signed Enrico Caruso, an Italian-American singer to the label; over time, this partnership released over 300 performance recordings. Victor became the most well-known recording label, ultimately causing the music industry to grow steadily. By 1910, the three largest record labels were Edison Records, Victor, and Columbia. Edison Records was known predominantly for its instrumental and symphonic compositions, and Columbia was associated with jazz and blues.

A mover and shaker in the early years of the Columbia Phonograph Company was an executive leader, Frank Walker, the founder of the 1920s music catalogs that contained genres of country, gospel, and blues recordings. According to Hardy, Walker initially recorded country music, previously called folk music, before moving on to record jazz and blues. Having notoriety as a talent scout in 1923, Hardy signed blues artist Bessie Smith and the singing accordionist Joseph Falcon in 1928. In 1938, Walker left Columbia and became the Vice President of what would become RCA-Victor. From there, the executive leader joined MGM, where he signed Hank Williams. After retiring, Walker became a consultant to MGM's parent company, Loew's Inc. In 1920, Victor became well-known as an international recording label when they signed and launched the career of Russian concert pianist Sergei Rachmaninoff.

RCA Victor is Born

In the 1920s, radio surpassed that of recorded music sales. People could now hear the news, sports, and political speeches, along with various types of entertainment, soap operas, and comedies. This prompted the decline of phonograph sales. Henceforth, RCA-Victor was born when Radio Corporation of America purchased Victor; the two companies became RCA-Victor. The company manufactured a radio and phonograph housed in a small cabinet, thereby forcing Edison to close the doors to his business and the label.

The Jukebox Challenges the Industry

In 1889, the jukebox was born although there is an accounting of the invention in England at the same time. An American, Louis T. Glass is credited with the. The jukebox was originally called the nickel-in-the-slot-machine and took a nickel to play a song. With the jukebox in restaurants, bars and clubs and becoming very popular, music sales began to increase once again. More than half of the music produced on record in the 1940s was for the jukebox as demand grew for new music during the World War II era (1939-1945), making the jukebox play a significant role in the history of the music industry.

In 1956 Wurlitzer manufactured a jukebox that played entire albums that increased revenue within the music industry. Joe Bihari, a pioneer in the music industry, bought blues genre records at 2 cents apiece to stock the jukeboxes and many times the stock did not supply the growing demand. Since records were sent to overseas troops, there was a change in the material used for production. Vinyl was then used to produce records because of a decrease in breakage when being shipped.

The AFM Strike for Pay

In 1942, musicians belonging to the American Federation of Musicians (AFM) went on strike under the direction of their leader, James Petrillo. During the war, musicians did not get paid when recordings played on the radio. Only the copyright owner received payment. Members of the union refused to play on recordings until the record labels agreed to pay them royalties. In 1944 the strike ended; until that time, artists had to perform with no instruments in the background. Artists such as Bing Crosby and Perry Como performed *a cappella* on numerous occasions.

Another famous event in the history of RCA-Victor was created in December 1948 when 10 famous artists recorded "I'm Just Wild About Harry." The recording company presented the recording to President Harry Truman. The recording ended an 11.5-month. The ban started because of musicians' complaints against recording companies, which consisted of claims that radio and juke box industries were getting the bulk of profits from the commercial use of musicians' recordings.

Changing Methods of Music Delivery

High fidelity recordings produced after the war produced a better-quality sound. Long playing albums entered the market as phonograph costs decreased. Recording companies would release a single to radio; if the single became a hit, the company would add other music tracks and release the album on the LP.

In the 1950s, tape recorders made editing simple and revolutionized the music industry. Artists and musicians until then had done their recordings live in the studio, and there was no way to correct errors, so they had to strive for perfection in their delivery. Once the tape recorder came into being, errors could be rectified by cutting out the errors—literally splicing the tape—and putting in the correction. Another feature was that each musician and artist could record on separate tracks, which could be spliced together at the end. If the artist or a musician was not present, their part could be added later to the recording of the session. Just as the mouse revolutionized the computer, so did four-track recorders change the music industry. In time, four-tracks were replaced by eight-tracks, and finally recorded digitally.

In the 1960s, the music industry went through another revolutionizing change as transistor radios, tape recorders and eight track tapes came on the horizon. The transistor was portable and could be carried in the palm of one's hand. Eight-track players became installed in Ford automobiles by 1965, but because they were too bulky, they became passé by 1970 and replaced with smaller cassette tapes. By 1968, 2.4 million cassette tapes were sold nationwide to households and installed in automobiles.

Payola

Executive leaders at recording organizations realized that repeated radio airplay was crucial to the success of their recorded product. As a means of increasing airplay, some companies invented payola. This was a system of paying radio announcers to play songs with more frequency. The Federal Communications Act amended in 1960 made accepting pay from recording labels for playing recorded music illegal for radio announcers.

MTV

As rock and roll music became more popular in the 1960s and 1970s, record sales increased to $1.2 billion. Recording companies such as Capital, Electra, Motown, and Atlantic Records emerged, along with motion picture businesses that used the soundtracks from the record companies. In 1981, a cable television channel known as Music Television (MTV) debuted to the market. Recording artists began to gain recognition on a national level because of video presentations on MTV

The channel entered New York and Los Angeles urban markets with songs by Michael Jackson. MTV was now facing debt, and possible closing began to see a profit by 1984. In turn, radio stations also started to profit due to Jackson's success. In December of 1983, Michael Jackson's video "Thriller" was launched on MTV, thereby saving the cable TV network from bankruptcy.

The CD Craze

The Sony Walkman, a handheld device for listening to cassette tapes, was introduced into the market and started a new trend in listening to music. By the early 1990s, millions of people were replacing their cassette tape collections with CDs and the players for their cars and homes along with portable CD players for carrying by hand. In 1999, CD music sales reached an excess of $38 million. In 2010 Sony stopped the manufacture and distribution of its popular Walkman due to consumer demand for CD players.

Napster: The Predecessor to Music Piracy

Ushering in a new threat to the music industry in the 21st century was the production of affordable CD burners for consumers that allowed free duplication of recorded music. Digital technology and the Internet became real threats to the music industry and traditional operations. Online music sharing sites such as Napster escalated the threat by helping consumers to download free music and share the music with millions of other users online.

With the influx of CD players, Napster—an MP3 peer-to-peer trading program—became the predecessor to waves of music piracy online. Ignoring this new era caused many companies to experience a decline in record sales and a limited understanding of what was happening to their organizations. The music industry changed considerably, due in part to free music download or to be more explicit, piracy using peer-to-peer services. With convenience being a primary factor and new technology on the horizon, a shift from purchasing licensed music to free digital downloads and the MP3 took place. Recorded audio files were compressed and saved into an MP3 format as opposed to the traditional .wav file. These compressed sound files allowed for more files to be stored and played on an MP3 player.

With the growing popularity of MP3 files, the MP3 player recording companies were not successful in gaining legislative support to control illegal downloading of music. On December 7, 1999, Napster—along with other websites providing free downloads of recorded music—was sued for copyright infringement by the Recording Industry Association of America.

Progression of the Digital Age

In 2001, Apple introduced the iPod, an MP3 player into the marketplace, providing customers with a device to store the massive MP3 music collections they were gathering. Although the device was produced to store music purchased from online locations such as iTunes, CD Baby, and other subscription services, piracy remained rampant online. RIAA estimated that more than 30 billion recorded songs downloaded for free by consumers; the sale of music decreased by 53% between 1999 and 2011. CDs were no longer popular with music fans as people became accustomed to downloading and listening to music digitally on their smartphones and other handheld devices such as the iPad and digital tablets. In addition, Internet radio provided convenience in listening to music. Consumers could customize to their music collections from music streaming sites such as Pandora and Spotify without having to download the music.

Maintaining the Legacy of Recorded Sound

The Recording Academy, formerly known as the National Academy of Recording Arts and Science (NARAS), honors artistic achievements, technical expertise, and excellence in the music industry. The Academy established itself as the distinguished advocate for the arts and as an outreach organization and consisting of managers, songwriters, singers, producers, engineers, and other music industry professionals by impacting the lives of not just musicians and members of the industry, but society. Because of its many efforts toward the preservation of musical art, music lovers and supporters reap great benefit. Each year, the Academy televises live recognition of the year's most exceptional talent in the music industry, covering every genre of music and spoken word.

Following suit for preservation, South by Southwest (SXSW) is the largest music festival in the world, taking place each year in Austin, Texas, offering nearly 3,000 live performances and advisory panels regarding the music industry and technology-based information and education throughout a 5-day span. The organization was launched in March 1987 and launched SXSW On ™ in 2015, a demand streaming network featuring and archiving performances and live talks.

In addition to these major music entities, just to list a sampling, are other organizations which are genre specific such as the Gospel Music Workshop of America (GMWA) which holds a major convention each year in various US cities to highlight and commemorate gospel music. The annual boards meeting held in march is culminated with the Annual Stellar Awards, celebrating the achievements of music artists; Gospel Music Association (GMA) which holds a major convention each year in Nashville to highlight and commemorate Christian Contemporary and Gospel Music. The three to four-day convention culminates with the well-known Dove Awards; The National Old Time Country, Bluegrass, and Folk Music Festival a weeklong festival celebrating music from the past and lifestyles of pioneers, their arts and their crafts. Participants include songwriters, pickers, and singers on ten stages.

Artists, Musicians, and Production

As technology allowed, independent artist began to use recording equipment such as Avid Pro Tools or Fruity Loops, now known as FL Studio 12, to create full instrumental and vocal recordings. For those proficient in using this digital technology the production software is less expensive than a studio engineer. Artists and musicians now had access to the Internet for distribution without having to sign a recording contract with a label. As a result, recording labels were forced to close their doors or were distributed under a bigger umbrella such as the "Big

Three": Warner Music Group, Sony BMG, and Universal Music Group. By 2012 the music industry's revenues fell by $16.5 billion.

Internet Music Sales

Further revolutionizing the music industry in 2001, Apple introduced iTunes software to the marketplace. The software allowed users to create their music and then manage the music on their personal computer. Initially, iTunes could only play and rip CDs to MP3, and then sync the music to MP3 players. Today, iTunes is a mega digital store offering music, videos, games, e-books, rentals, and more. iTunes also houses the App Store. After illegal music piracy almost destroyed the music industry, iTunes proved that downloaded music was not only desirable but profitable. Industry sales began to climb, and artists and musicians looked to iTunes for distribution of their music as opposed to seeking out a recording label to record and provide distribution.

CD Baby

As an alternative to the recording company and traditional distribution sources and out of the frustration of executive leaders, musicians and recording artists came an online music distribution source called CD Baby. The distributor provided over 850 music genres and distributed music by independent artists from all over the world. To the dismay of music industry personnel at recording companies, artist could now record their music and distribute the product online with marketing resources available to them.

Social Media Explosion

The explosion of social media connected the world in ways that were previously unheard-of. Social media provided people with the ability to share information on the Internet in ways never dreamed. As the world was adjusting to the medium of email transmissions for real-time communication, chat rooms were introduced. The social networking explosion came in the form of MySpace, Facebook, Twitter, YouTube, Instagram, Pinterest, LinkedIn, Quora, Google Plus, Flickr, Ryze, TalkBiznow, Affluence, SnapChat, bulk email texting, and many others. Despite the plethora of digital tools available, leaders required an extensive understanding of digital know-how to compete with this broad range of resources. A handful of executives begin utilizing these resources but for the most part music industry personnel were not yet utilizing this powerful medium of communication to gain added exposure for the company or the artist. In the past, recording companies and their marketing departments could control the artists' image with their fan base due to traditional distribution through retail outlets. Social media, however, enabled the artist to become integrated with the culture and humanized in the eyes of fans. This broadened the relationship between the artist and his or her fans.

Social Media Platform

A social media platform is a network of social media tools such as Facebook, Twitter, Instagram, Pinterest, LinkedIn, SnapChat and Google hosted in one place for quality control by the company. Examples of social media software that manages a social media platform are HootSuite Pro, ManageFlitter, Google Analytics, Monday.com and NUVI which are designed to manage these networks, promote the company's brand, and measure the performance of those social media networks used with reports that create with analytics. Analytic data allow executive leadership to make informed business and marketing decisions. A tech-savvy executive leader would benefit from this software in tracking clients' mobility and performance.

The primary role of a social media platform is to enhance the company's sense of community and to grow the business by listening to the customer as they respond within the company's social media network. The platform provides a viable experience for the music fan or customer. In turn, the social media platform provides a means for the company to respond to the client via the platform.

There are core components of the social media platform. They are social media channels that provide community services that create awareness and connect supporters, mixing with outside social media channels, and adding a live feed of the company's social media networks to its company website. After determining the tools to be used to market and promote the social media platform, a company must decide who would be responsible for maintaining the network and whether the resource would be retained in-house or outsourced. Available time, budget, and expertise all play a part in this decision.

Social Media and the Executive Leader

Regarding social media, leaders require a more extensive selection of style alternatives to match the more extensive range of resources that companies are creating today. The executive leader who works hand-in-hand with fans, customers, and artists to achieve the goals of the company can tap into the originality and resourcefulness of people utilizing social media opportunities. This promotes a wealth of new knowledge and resources. The executive leader who engages in a co-creative style has been shown to grow faster and become more accessible and lucrative than those who do not step out of the box of in-house and branded solutions.

Executive leaders who employ digital strategies recognize that there are challenges associated with this domain. Leaders must understand the relationship they have with the artist, music fans, customers, and partners to determine how they want those links to look in the future. The executive leader recognizes his or her deepest fears when giving up control and can visualize what opportunities are forthcoming when they do.

Music Streaming

In 2016 media streaming made up 34.3% of sales, surpassing digital downloads regarding revenue. Music could now be delivered over the Internet in real time to computers and digital devices. The free-for-all model for piracy was interrupted by iTunes technology, causing music download technology improvements by music industry start-ups and innovators. As a result, companies such as Spotify, SoundCloud, Beats Electronic, and Pandora were born.

Pandora became the industry leader, becoming neck in neck with Spotify, in music live streaming, causing iTunes to experience declining sales. When Apple experienced a late release of Apple Music, this presented a greater opportunity to maintain and increase Pandora's new artist and subscription base. In 2015, Pandora paid royalties to record labels, performing rights organizations, and publishers to aid in Pandora's global expansion and on-demand service. To connect listeners with live events, the company also purchased Ticketfly for $450 million. Since the collapse in the music industry, almost two decades ago, the industry saw positive signs of growth in 2016 with revenue up by 8.1% for record labels due to music streaming subscribers. Downloads were down by 14% and physical product sales down by 17% with music streaming up by 57%.

Those most affected by the decrease in sales and eventual downsizing of recording companies were music industry personnel and company personnel, engineers, producers, songwriters, radio, and retail and print media professionals. Despite artists being able to record and distribute their music, there remained a deficit in artists' concert bookings and live performances. With live streaming gaining notoriety, artists were being heard, but performance bookings were still down. There is still an essential need for music industry personnel with digital strategies. According to Light who ranked number 9 in the Top 100 Music Very Important Persons of 2015, live performances are where the money is for artists and musicians.

According to Light, the top breakout artists got there because of touring; people still want to see and hear artists live and in person.

Executive leaders stopped comparing the industry to the Titanic and defining as a sinking ship and began to embrace it. Music industry personnel had to step away from traditional album sales practices in their thinking. As social media and streaming technology became more prolific, recording artists discovered that they could now bypass traditional record labels for exposure to the marketplace. Many of them began utilizing social media venues to gain the exposure needed to market their product.

The history illustrates the challenges associated with changing technology and reveals that the music industry has successfully weathered many such changes before. The review of the industry, however, also revealed a gap in research regarding the digital strategies needed to lead a successful recorded music organization.

Mastering digital strategies requires the ability to successfully navigate, gauge, and generate information using an array of digital technologies to achieve important aims. Being digitally literate is an ongoing process in which individuals must consistently and actively try new technology tools and resources, build strategies with these techniques, and use these technologies to meet their needs and achieve their goals. When individuals consistently keep up with technology, learn new digital resources, and effectively use these skills, they are exercising the ongoing process of digital literacy.

Summary

A review of history revealed many setbacks and changes that the music industry has undergone over the course of 100+ years. From the invention of the phonograph to live music streaming on the Internet, the challenges and changes that have taken place over the past 100+ years are not new to the industry, just different. The technology of the day has always been the catalyst for the changes that took place. With each change came a more improved method of delivery or visibility. Music industry personnel at record companies suffered significant losses yet retained incredible options for survival within the industry. As music industry personnel embrace new technology and the resources provided, companies can again enjoy the successes of the past, but with a new engine of technology and social media.

Those affected by the digital strategies and the changing dynamics of the music industry include the recording companies, who gain greater access to fans and increased distribution methods. Digital strategies allow performing artists and musicians to reap the benefits of extended booking tours, broader promotion, and greater marketing exposure. Radio stations benefit by downloading the music directly from the recording company, rather than obtaining a physical product. Ultimately, the consumer reaps benefits such as greater ease of purchase through online downloads.

Becoming proficient in digital skills and strategies involves knowledge, competency, and a new way of thinking to operate successfully. Digital literacy is an ongoing process and must consistently be kept up with by actively learning and trying out new technology tools and resources, building strategies with these techniques, and using these technologies to meet needs and achieve goals. When consistency is maintained with technology and digital resources and tools and using strategies, it is possible to achieve digital literacy.

CHAPTER THREE – SKILLS & STRATEGIES

First things first

So, you've produced a song or an album. All the songs have been copyrighted (protected) and belong exclusively to you or your signed artists. As a sole proprietor of your music or a company representing the work of others, you've established a music publishing company and business license; you've registered with a performing rights organization such as BMI, ASCAP, SESAC who collect license fees on your behalf and in turn distribute royalties to you when your works have been performed. You've registered your music to be sold and distributed to digital music streaming services such as Spotify, Pandora, Google Play and many others at sites such as CDBaby.com, or Landr.com. You are ready to share your talent with the world as a recorded music company or independent artist. Where do you go from there? Let's discuss some available options.

Radio

Don't rule out radio stations because of the digital revolution. They are still a very key element in the success of your music product. Although many local stations once listened too may be off the air, there are still many who are still airing and are also live streaming on the internet to the rest of the world. Send your product along with a press kit to not just your local stations who represent your market but to stations in key cities. If you have a brief video of your performance this will add to your acceptance by the stations and the word will get out. The product has to be professional and not a homemade production. Make sure the product gets to the right person, so find out who the programmer for your genre of music is. Remember, every announcer is not a programmer. Do your research. Another viable source in radio is SiriusXM. Send a package to the Music Programming Department. In the press kit which can include a biography explaining the sound and accomplishments of you or your group, a professional photo, a compact demo disc of no more than three of your songs in mp3 format. Including your social media address is an additional aid for the programmer to get to know you, your group, or your company. Include a cover letter and how to reach you. And to help the programmer, suggest channels on SiriusXM that you want your music to be played on. This means of course knowing the music content of the channels requested. Do the research.

Once the music and press kit are distributed to the stations whether manually or digitally and the music is in rotation at the station, you'll want to develop a relationship with the announcer(s) playing your music. Track the product on a weekly basis to see how it's being received in the market and to know whether it's being played and how heavy or light the rotation is. Once a relationship is developed with the station and the product is in rotation the potential for concert bookings in that city becomes a stronger possibility.

Social Media Marketing - Strategy

Social media has been the greatest innovation of technology in terms of communication and marketing. Knowing which platforms to use is important to achieving goals. Being familiar with what each media platform offers is key to choosing the right ones. Each social media platform changes and updates their site periodically to provide greater advantages and security to its users therefore constant research of updates is crucial to staying on top of what you may or may not be able to provide to your "friends" base. Although there are several platforms on the Internet only a few will be shared here.

Facebook provides not only the opportunity to connect with friends and fans but vendors, radio, and retail by matching them with similar prospects with similar characteristics. Facebook allows photos, and video and provides live streaming and the ability to move perspective buyers of the product or service to a page whereby they can provide your company with their name and email.

Twitter posts are known just as Facebook to go viral and the more people share your post the more followers you gain. When people or companies have many followers, retweeting them increases your following when others see your posts and thereby providing you with more names to market to. Twitter only requires a line or two of text to get the message out and can include a picture or video to enhance the message.

LinkedIn was originally designed as a business to business (B2B) site and provides connection between business professionals. Although the site serves several purposes Groups are a key part of its connection strategy in that an artist can literally build a network inviting other artists, promoters, marketing managers and others involved in the music industry on LinkedIn and host online forums which help to enlighten, strengthen and unify the group.

Instagram is designed to share photos and videos via your smartphone or any IOS or Android device. Instagram's purpose is to provide value to your followers with vibrant colors and videos to get more engagement from them. Adding simple brief hashtags is a great way to increase activity of followers. It's important to note that when an Instagram video, which can last for up to an hour ends, it goes away for good and does not replay as in Facebook. Followers may want to ensure they are there to watch so as not to miss what's being offered. It could be a concert performance or a live interview, or video-conferencing a small office meeting.

You Tube provides local and cable television stations online by offering varying bundles for pay. You Tube is primarily a video sharing service where users can both watch and create their own channels that users can subscribe to. Users can find video topics on practically any subject for free on You Tube. For a small fee by the You Tube subscriber, commercials can be restricted from any You Tube video to ensure there are no interruptions while viewing. You tube is a great audio/visual marketing tool for artists and managers who want to increase artist and/or product visibility and branding.

Pinterest provides creative inspiration in that it allows pinners (you) to post new information about their product in specific categories (ie: music). Clicking on a picture of a new music release cover could literally send a user to your website or to another page that has say a profile about the artist or the company. For example, a booking tour schedule could be saved as a graphic file (picture) and thereby providing the user with the artist's tour dates at a glance. The user can in turn re-pin any picture back to Pinterest and thereby alerting more users to that graphic. If your goal is brand awareness then a tool like BoardBooster which recycles your pins may be a huge help in optimizing your strategy, cleaning up your boards, scheduling pins and improving pin quality.

Every business or individual has to have goals. Setting goals is the staple of all marketing strategy. For example, focusing on meaningful content and strong branding through your social media channels can increase brand awareness. Through social media targeting you can reach your target market much quicker. Creating a loyal fan base by promoting user-generated content that your fans can react to positively may possibly be some of your goals. Marketing strategy is crucial to the success of your business or career therefore creating social media goals is key toward your success. I learned at an early age to document everything that I want to see happen from time management to goal setting. I found that I was more apt to achieve the goal when I wrote it down as opposed to when I didn't.

Choose the social media platforms you will use and research the audience. According to research, Facebook users are comprised of approximately 79% adults and Instagram users are reported to be 59% 18-29 year old. Forty five percent of the members on LinkedIn had annual earnings of $75,000 or more whereas Snapchat demographics showed that 27% of its users earned less than $50,000 and 56% were 18-29 years old.

Social Media Analytics and Management

To provide an overview of who is following your social media and how they interact with you a social media dashboard is necessary. A social media dashboard such as HootSuite, Monday.com, or Google Analytics manages multiple accounts in one location. These necessary tools allow you to track how far your social media channels are reaching; how long and how often the users are engaging in the website. It allows you to get a view of the traffic to the site, when and how often. It further shows how many leads are being generated, whether there are any who have signed up for membership or other sign-up events and it shows how much revenue has been generated. The dashboard meshes the social networks together and inspects the information per social media channel or as a group. It analyzes posts, hashtags, user engagement and sentiment. The dashboard gets a birds-eye view of your social media calendar in order to schedule content on time without having to pull something together last minute. Time management is critical, and the dashboard organizes posting dates and times efficiently. This keeps from having to post with no rhyme or reason, thereby weakening the presence online. Its critical to know and understand when the best times are to post social media online. To help brands prepare for future campaigns its critical to know which keywords are trending and what hashtags are used most often from posts.

The website - Strategy

Ten to fifteen years ago everyone was trying to build a website but abandoned ship when social media became popular as an effective means of communication. Many are still tooting their horn via a website and doing it quite effectively. Of course there are those who feel it sufficient to rely solely on social media networks to get their music message to the world. Why would you let social media be your only outlet for exposure when you can be the horn and the horn blower? BUILD A WEBSITE!!! Integrate the two. How else will you develop effective strategy? How else will you build your brand? It doesn't matter if you are a multi-billion-dollar company or Joe Singer-Man needing to get his career off the ground and be successful at it. The most valuable piece of your marketing strategy is your website and your social media.

Having a company or a career in the music industry without a website is like being homeless and inviting others to come visit. Where do they go? BUILD A WEBSITE!!! There are hundreds of web developers in the market from Network Solutions.com to Go Daddy.com but if you're on a shoestring budget try online companies such as Wix.com or Wordpress.com which will help you establish your personal or company identity, your domain, and provide tools to build the site yourself, until you can afford to upgrade.

What target market are you going after? Your website should be reflective of the primary market you want to attract. What is your brand? Will your website identify and give you a major edge over others in the business with a significant name or company title, logo, or even the quality of music product you want to sell?? The site should be reflective of your brand. It should be up to date always and easy for users to navigate and find what your site advertises and claims to be there whether its services, video, product for sale, or a simple contact page.

Search Engine Optimization (SEO) - Strategy

Once your web site is up and running you'll want to make sure its fully perfect, or at least close to perfect, functional and effective as it can possibly be. In other words that it is optimized. We then look at search engine optimization which is the practice of increasing the quality and the quantity of traffic to your website through search engine results that don't have to be paid for. Optimizing a website means developing it to become highly visible to search. A key is that the title of the site is keyword based and the pages of the site are all listed. Optimizing is to create meta tags which are extracts of text describing the contents of the web page. Meta tags are not seen by the user but is code imbedded on the page describing to the search engines what the page is about. Search engines can determine if the meta tags represent what is actually on the page. Placing strategic search words and phrases on each page also optimizes and enhances the site. Finally, linking your URL with key directories such as DMOZ, Yahoo Directory or Google is important because it links your website with the directory and ultimately allows people to find your pages easily. Linking provides credibility to your website especially if the site you're linked to has high visibility. Your primary goal is to get to the top of the search engines.

Become familiar with Google and the various tools offered to track and analyze a website. With increased traffic to a website the pages have the potential to get a ranking number from 1 -10 in Google™ when other web pages are linked to them. When the site has great and relevant content in the words and phrases, a descriptive title, relevant keywords, and links that connect to related pages, others will want to link to your pages. When others have linked to your site and shared the link, this moves your ranking up in Google. When you in turn link to theirs as well you strengthen your sites chances of ranking higher. Of course, the site that links to you has to be of quality. This in turn makes your website easy to find in search engines such as Google, Yahoo, and Bing. Have you ever wondered why some sites are at the top of the list in search engines and some are unable to be found at all? SEO is all about moving the site to the top of the search engine page, so people can find the website and click. A good reference source of do's and don'ts titled How To Get To Number 1 On Google in 2018 Without Breaking the Rules can be found on the Internet.

Marketing Analytics

Marketing analytics is a major part of your digital strategies and lets you know how your marketing and promotion strategies are really performing. If you have not added or are using social media analytics, then you are more than likely frustrated because you don't know how your top performing Tweets, Facebook, Pinterest, Instagram, or other social media posts are performing. You may not know whether your marketing strategy for Facebook or other media posts are bringing in traffic and leads or what time of day your social media posts are getting the greatest amount of traffic. Social media analytics tools are available all over the Internet. These tools are available for analysis of websites only or analysis of websites and social media. Some are tools to analyze social media only. For instance, a tool such as Buzzsumo analyses your website performance on social media whereas Google Analytics tracks social media campaigns and measures how efficient the campaigns are. While tracking your social media performance Google Analytics creates reports that you can access. If you have set-up You Tube videos to earn revenue, then you will want to utilize analytics tools to track the video product. You'll want to know if people are clicking on the video but not watching the video; how many are watching and whether they came from a website or search engine, and more. No money is made from the click. Money is made when they watch the video for 30 seconds or more. Therefore, in addition to tools that track all of your social media platforms there are tools that also include analysis of your YouTube videos. Tools such as Quintly, Simply Measured and Rival IQ are a few that are offered. All of this sounds a bit tedious but is actually quite simple in application. The key is deciding which analytics tool to use and whether you want to purchase the tool or use the free versions offered. There is of course another route and that is hiring someone or a firm to do it all for you. Knowing what is required gives you the upper hand in being able to hold them accountable for performance and delivery.

Driving the Car

Now that you have gassed up and you have your strategies in place and you know where you want to go, it's time to turn on the engine and begin driving. If you're a new driver, take a test drive to get use to driving the car. As you become more proficient at driving you can then begin to expand your knowledge on how to drive the car more efficiently and with greater results. Stay abreast of new technology, knowing it changes frequently. Remember when recorded videos were bombarding space on Facebook? Now live streaming is common place on all social media platforms. Collecting royalties, online tracking, sales and payments are commonplace. Old school practices are not a thing of the past as some might believe. Many of the old-school practices are still being implemented but todays digital standards coupled with some old school practices will still get you miles ahead of the game as you use this digital blueprint for music industry success.

ABOUT THE AUTHOR

Dr. Joyce Logan has over 40 years of experience in the entertainment industry and a proven record of success with some of the top names in gospel music. She created the leading music trade site on the Internet and the nation's leading music trade magazine for the Gospel and Christian Community. Her efforts resulted in the world-wide internet debut of Gospel International in October of 1994. Initially, she used the basic magazine-newsletter content she had created and sent out to industry executives as the first step of her overall marketing strategy to launch Gospel International Online. Dr. Logan continued to gather and create the necessary files incorporated into her internet site although the Internet was still in its infancy. Over a two-year period, she expanded her presence online while continuing to perfect the appearance and information presented which resulted in Gospel International becoming one of the leading Gospel-Christian Sites on the Internet. Developing the framework for a multi-media gospel enterprise combining traditional "street level experience" with "technology" based delivery systems, her ability to respond to the changing marketplace using technology is an example why Dr. Logan remains "cutting edge". She maintains ongoing relationships with leading music industry executives, community and national organizations, musical artists. While attaining the rank of Sergeant in the U.S. Army, she served three years as a Telecommunications Center Specialist Instructor at Fort Gordon, Georgia. During this time, she was invited to sing with the gospel group James Bignon & God's Children. As both lead and background singer, the group appeared on major concert dates with such noted artists as Shirley Caesar, The Mighty Clouds of Joy, Rev. James Cleveland, and many others. Dr. Logan gained recognition for her broad vocal range and accepted invitations to sing "studio" background vocals for many popular artists. As a songwriter, she "penned" such noted songs that achieved Billboard Magazine's top Gospel chart "status". After her tour of military duty ended, she attended the noted Columbia School of Broadcasting, from which she graduated with honors. In 1983, she accepted a position as Gospel Editor of Black Radio Exclusive Magazine (BRE), a leading music industry publication where she established and maintained its first gospel music section. Her Gospel section, the only one of its kind in America, became a highly popular feature. As a direct result of its increasing popularity, Dr. Logan set the standard for many of today's gospel music magazines. The departments under her direction were; "National News Briefs," "VIP Spotlight," "The Top 20 Gospel Chart," "Gospel Record Reviews," "Gospel Retail and Radio Reports," and "Gospel Commentary. Through technology she created the "standard" to communicate the Gospel-Christian message to millions of people.

Ms. Logan was invited to join Word, Inc. (then a division of ABC/Capital Cities Broadcasting), the nation's largest Christian communications company. In 1989, after coordinating the world premiere of Shirley Caesar's (award-winning) video, Hold My Mule, she was asked by WORD to serve as Assistant Marketing Director, under gospel music industry mogul and pioneer, James Bullard. She was soon promoted to the position of Marketing Director and, in a short time, assumed the position of A&R Administrator, working in both capacities concurrently. Her responsibilities included; development and implementation of artist marketing and promotional plans for Shirley Caesar, Al Green, Milton Brunson & Thompson Community Singers, DeLeon Richards, The Clark Sisters, Albertina Walker, The Mighty Clouds of Joy, O'Landa Draper, The Richard Smallwood Singers, Daniel Winans, and The Brooklyn Tabernacle Choir, to name a few. She was responsible for devising overall sales strategy and determining how the artist's product would be positioned in the marketplace. She worked closely with the art department in developing materials used by the sales staff. She coordinated all convention plans for her division and implemented those plans successfully at and during major conferences and conventions). She was responsible for coordinating sales conferences for her division and on occasion was the primary speaker during the conference. She was responsible for setting up TV interviews or appearances on major television networks. As A&R Administrator, she worked very closely with producers and session venues in every aspect of the recording process including; carefully monitoring the budget of each artist during both pre-production and post-production cycles, setting up the recording venue and any additional artistic needs of the producer for the session, coordinated travel and lodging arrangements for the artists during a recording cycle. Her work also included artist development, maintaining artist itineraries, coordinating artist's promotional tours, development and maintenance of systematic contact and rapport with major media sources along with interacting daily with radio announcers and retailers across the country.

She accepted a temporary marketing assignment with Chicago-based CGI Records, (a division of the large Platinum Entertainment Group) where her display of commitment and strategy resulted in CGI receiving nationwide recognition and substantial chart action for the label's recordings. Within three months the company moved from no prominence to high visibility within the gospel music industry.

After leaving CGI Dr. Logan founded Gospel International. Her understanding and "vision" driven by her entrepreneurial spirit made her dream a reality. Dr. Logan envisioned Gospel International going out to millions of households and businesses around the world via the Internet before it was popular or practical. She made it her "business" (while supporting the development stages of Gospel International by independent consulting) to simultaneously become an expert in computer technology and the Internet.

Dr. Logan continues to spend a great deal of time researching the latest technology and software in leading computer trade publications, seminars and workshops. She has surrounded herself with individuals who would be considered computer-programming specialists and social media marketing gurus, who also keep her informed of the latest software and technological advances being made.

Dr. Logan is a member of the Association of Black Women Entrepreneurs, the National Association for Female Executives, The Advertising Research Foundation, Black Business Entrepreneurs Association, and the American Society of Magazine Editors. Dr. Logan is a registered songwriter with BMI (Broadcast Music International), the largest and oldest music licensing organizations in America.

On Christmas day 1999 Gospel International was severely hacked online and the publication was sabotaged. After months of attempts at trying to restore all that had been destroyed Dr. Logan lost everything and ended up in a homeless shelter for almost a year. In 2006 she launched Gospel International Video Magazine and it became very successful. In 2008 the online site was again sabotaged. Determined to regain all that she'd lost and become even more proficient at what she could do for others within the industry, she underwent major living sacrifices and went back to school achieving a bachelor's degree in Information Technology, MBA in Marketing, and her Doctorate in Management with a concentration in Executive Leadership.

Her ongoing desire is to provide quality information and resources to the music industry once again considering the industry collapse which affected recording companies, management teams, promoters, artists and songwriters nationwide. Seeing the desperate need for the entire music industry in every genre to regain its lost footing she has structured this book to become a motivational and educational manual for all desiring direction and ultimately, success.

Ms. Logan shares this book with the world to motivate, educate, and enlighten those in need of getting their businesses and careers off the ground either once again or initially, and flowing successfully. Her goal is to provide a blueprint for digital SUCCESS. She currently provides skills and strategies training in live workshops and seminars to both businesses and faith based orgaizations. Although the music industry is the target for reference in this book, the skills and strategies apply to any business or organization.

By Hillary Hicks

THE RESEARCH - REFERENCES

Abrahamsen, M. H. (2016). Researching business interaction: introducing a conceptual framework and methodology. *IMP Journal*, 10(3), 464-482.

AFM. (2016). *Dont go it alone*. Retrieved from American Federationof Musicians: http://www.afm.org/about/about-afm/

Aggarwal, R. (2011). Developing a global mindset: Integrating demographics, sustainability, technology, and globalization. *Journal of Teaching in International Business*, 22(1), 51-69.

Alyahya, M. (2012, February). Changing organizational structure and organizational memory in primary care practices: a qualitative interview study. *Health Services Managment Research*, pp. 25(1), 35-40.

AOL. (2015). Retrieved from AOL.com: http://www.aol.com/

Apple. (2016). *iTunes Previews*. Retrieved from iTunes: https://itunes.apple.com/us/genre/ios/id36?mt=8

Atkin, J. L., & McCardle, M. (2015, October). Old Dog, New Tricks: Staying Relevant in the Digital Era. *Journal of Critical Incidents*, pp. 8, 77-80.

Awad, G. (2014). Motivation, Persistance, and Crosscultural Awareness: A study of College Students Learning Foreign Languages. *Academy of Educational Leadership Journal*, pp. 18(4), 97-116.

Baby, C. (2016). *CD Baby:the best independent music store on the web*. Retrieved from CD Baby: The biggest little online record store: http://www.cdbaby.com/about

Bae, S., & Asojo, A. (2016). An exploratory study focused on movements and interactions in the work environment. *ArchNet-IJAR*, 10(2), 192-203.

Bandow, D., & Self, T. B. (2016, November). Leadership at all Levels: Developing Managers to Develop Leaders. *Journal of International Business Disciplines*, pp. 11(2), 60-74.

Baran, B., Shanock, L., & Miller, L. (2012). Advancing Organizational Support Theory into the Twenty-First Century World of Work. *Journal of Business & Psychology*, 27 (2) 123-147.

Basch, M. (1992, February). Wired for sound: Digital Cable Radio makes debut. *Florida Times Union*.

Baschab, J., & Piot, J. (2007). *The Executive's Guide to Information Technology (2nd Ed.)*. Hoboken, N.J.: Wiley.

Bellows-Riecken, K., Mark, R., & Rhodes, R. E. (2013, September). Qualitative elicitation of affective beliefs related to physical activity. *Psychology of Sport & Exercise*, pp. 14(5), 786-792.

Bihari, J. (2012). Modern Records: A Conversation with Joe Bihari. ARSC Journal. Vol. 43 Issue 1, p66-75. 10p. (J. Brovan, Interviewer)

Bing, D. (2012). The Weakness of Strong Leaders: Crowding Out Space for Collective Purpose. *People & Strategy*, pp. 35, 36-61.

Bishop, L. (2012). Using archived qualitative data for teaching: practical and ethical considerations. *International Journal of Social Research Methodology*, 15 (4) 341-350.

Blandford, A. (2013). Semi-Structured Qualitative Studies. *The Encyclopedia of Human-Computer Interaction, 2nd Ed.*

Boehlert, E. (1994). Put another nickel in. *Billboard*, 106(44), 93.

Borchers, A., Cellucci, L. W., Hodge, K., & Peters, C. (2016). Case Writer's Workshop. *Journal of Case Studies*, 34(1), 1-10.

Bottomley, A. J. (2015). Home taping is killing music': the recording industries' 1980s anti-home taping campaigns and struggles over production, labor and creativity. *Creative Industries Journal*, 8(2), 123-145.

Bottomley, K., Burgess, S., & Fox III, M. (2014). Are the Behaviors of Transformational Leaders Impacting Organizations? A Study of Transformational Leadership. *International Management Review*, pp. 10(1), 5-9.

Bourne, A. H., & Robson, M. A. (2015). Participants' reflections on being interviewed about risk and sexual behaviour: implications for collection of qualitative data on sensitive topics. *International Journal of Social Research Methodology*, 18(1), 105-116.

Brinkmann, S. (2014). Interview. In S. Brinkmann, *Encyclopedia of Critical Psychology* (pp. pp 1008-1010). New York: Springer.

Brooks, T. (2013). 360 Sound: The Columbia Records Story/Columbia Records: Pioneer in Recorded Sound: America's Oldest Record Company, 1886 to the Present. *ARSC Journal*, 44(1), 130-134.

Bruno, A. (2011). The NARAS Network. *Billboard*, 123(5), 12-12.

Budden, C. R., Svechnikova, K., & White, J. (2017, February). Why do surgeons teach? A qualitative analysis of motivation in excellent surgical educators. *Medical Teacher*, pp. 39(2), 188-194.

Burkus, D. (2010). *Skills Theory*. Retrieved from DAvid Burkus: http://davidburkus.com/2010/02/skills-theory/

Cameron, K. (2011). Responsible leadership as virtuous leadership. *Journal of Business Ethics*, 98, 25-35.

Casebeer. (2013, November 23). *Today in History – The First Jukebox Made It's Musical Debut*. Retrieved from American Blues Scene Magazine: https://www.americanbluesscene.com/2013/11/today-in-history-the-first-jukebox-made-its-debut/

Caven, V. (2012). Agony aunt, hostage, intruder or friend? The multiple personas of the interviewer during fieldwork. *Intangible Capital*, 8(3), 548-563.

Chandler, M. (2016, March 23). Apple Music Rival Pandora Spending More To Boost Its Lean Forward. *Investor's Business Daily*.

Chaney, D. (2012). The Music Industry in the Digital Age: Consumer Participation in Value Creation. *International Journal of Arts Management*, pp. 15(1), 42-52.

Charrow, R. (2007). Protection of human subjects: Is expansive regulation counter-productive? *Northwestern University Law Review*, 101(2), 707-721.

Chesebro, J. W., Foulger, D. S., Naghman, J. E., & Yannelli, A. (1985). Popular music as a mode of communication, 1955–1982. *Critical Studies in Mass Communication*, 2(2), 115-135.

Chowdhury, M. F. (2015). Coding, sorting and sifting of qualitative data analysis: debates and discussion. *Quality and Quantity*, 1135-1143.

Christman, E. (1995, July 29). NRM to stay out of retail wars. *Billboard*, pp. Vol. 107, (30), 81.

Close-Up Media, I. (2008). Sony BMG Now 100% Owned by Sony. *Wireless News*.

Cojocaru, C., & Cojocaru, S. (2014). Sony vs. Apple - iPod launching, a case study of leadership and innovation. *Manager*, 115-125.

Collins, C. S., & Cooper, J. E. (2014). Emotional Intelligence and the Qualitative Researcher. *International Journal of Qualitative Methods*, pp. 13, 88-103.

Collins, M. (2004). *Pro Tools for Music Production: Recording, Editing and Mixing 2nd Edition*. Burlington MA: Focal Press.

Company, T. P. (2013, October 17). *In 1919 the Radio Corporation of America, or RCA, was created*. Retrieved from Orlando Sentinel: http://search.proquest.com.proxy.cecybrary.com/docview/1442450623?accountid=45927

Context, B. i. (2006). *Emile Berliner: World of Invention*. Retrieved from Gale: http:www.galegroup.com/apps/doc/K1647000030/BIC1?u=tec_u_online&xid=a3dd671

Corp, I. D. (2010, April). Digital information to grow to thirty-five trillion gigabytes by 2020. Are you ready? *IM@T.Online*, p. 13.

Costas, R., Leeuwen, T. N., & Bordons, M. (2012). Referencing patterns of individual researchers: Do top scientists rely on more extensive information sources? *Journal of the American Society for Information Science & Technology*., 63(12), 2433-2450.

Cox, I. (2014). CIOs should spend more time building knowledge outside the IT department. *Computer Weekly*, 13.

Cresswell, J. (2014). *Research Design (4th Ed.)*. Thoussand Oaks, California: Sage.

Cunnama, L., & Honda, A. (2016, November 21). A mother's choice: a qualitative study of mothers' health seeking behaviour for their children with acute diarrhoea. *BMC Health Services Research*, pp. 16, 1-11.

Curtis, D. A., Lind, S. L., Boscardin, C. K., & Dellinges, M. (2013, June). Does student confidence on multiple-choice question assessments provide useful information? *Medical Education*, pp. 47(6), 578-584.

Cusumano, M. A. (2011). Technology Strategy and Management Platform Wars Come to Social Media. *Communications of the ACM*, 54(4), 31-33.

Dahl, B. (2015). The Birth of Top 40 Radio: The Storz Stations' Revolution of the 1950s and 1960s/Payola in the Music Industry: A History, 1880-1991. *ARSC Journal*, 312-313, 339. Retrieved from The Birth of Top 40 Radio: The Storz Stations' Revolution of the 1950s and 1960s/Payola in the Music Industry: A History, 1880-1991.

Davenport, B. (2014). From A to google: How technology is impacting information and leadership. *Journal of Leadership Studies*, 8(2), 41-45.

Deagon, B. (2016). Amazon Takes On Apple, Spotify, Pandora With Music Streaming Plan. *Investors Business Daily*, 1.

Deschamps, J.-P. (2008). *Innovation Leaders: How Senior Executives Stimulate, Steer and Sustain Innovation* . San Francisco, CA: Jossey-Bass.

Di Rosa, E., & Giunchiglia, E. (2013). Combining approaches for solving satisfiability problems with qualitative preferences. *AI Communications*, 26(4), 395-408.

DiGiacomo, F. (2016, February 2). The 100 Power. *Billboard*, p. 128(5).

DIJK, J. A. (2012). *IOS Press*. Retrieved from The Evolution of the Digital Divide The Digital Divide turns to Inequality of Skills and Usage: https://www.utwente.nl/en/bms/vandijk/news/The%20Evolution%20of%20the%20Digital%20Divide/Evolution%20of%20the%20Digital%20Divide%20Digital%20Enlightment%20Yearbook%202012.pdf

Dongen, M. A. (2014, May/June). Toward a Standardized Model for Leadership Development in International Organizations. *Global Business & Organizational Excellence*, pp. 33(4), 6-17.

Doody, O., & Noonan, M. (2013, May). Preparing and conducting interviews to collect data. *Nurse Researcher*, pp. 20(5), 28-32.

Dries, N., & Pepermans, R. (2012, May/June). How to identify leadership potential: Development and testing of a consensus model. *Human Resource Management*, pp. 51(3), 361-385.

Dubbels, K. (2015). The Piracy Crusade: How the Music Industry's War on Sharing Destroys Markets and Erodes Civil Liberties. *Library Quarterly*, 85(3), 339-342.

Dura, C., & Driga, I. (2011). The use of ranking sampling within marketing research. *Annals of the University of Petrosani Economics.* , 11(1), 77-88.

Eblin, S. (2011). *The Next Level: What Insiders Know About Executive Success, (2nd ed.).* Biston London: Nicholas Brealey Publishing.

Edie, P. C. (2016). *An overview of the phonographs of the victor talking machine company*. Retrieved from The Victor-Victrola Page: http://www.victor-victrola.com/

Editors. (2016). *Phonograph: Record Player*. Retrieved from Encyclopaedia Britanica: https://www.britannica.com/technology/phonograph

Ellis, T. (2004). Music is What it's all about. *Music Week*, 27.

Emerson, K. A. (2002). Dealing with the internal effects of a downsizing. *Business NH Magazine*, 19, (5), 32.

Entertainment, S. M. (2012). *The columbia records story: An interactive timeline*. Retrieved from Columbia Records: http://www.columbiarecords.com/timeline/#!date=1882-11-09_08:17:04!

E-Scan. (2013). Digital age is transforming leadership skills. *E-Scan Newsletter*, 39(3), 1.

Ewen, C., Wihler, A., Frieder, R. E., Blickle, G., Hogan, R., & Ferris, G. R. (2014). Leader Advancement Motive, Political Skill, Leader Behavior, and Effectiveness: A Moderated Mediation Extension of Socioanalytic Theory. *Human Performance*, 27(5), 373-392.

Farkus, A. (1997). *Enrico Caruso: My Father and My Family*. Portland, Oregon: Amadeus Press.

Farrell, M. (2015, February/March). Long Term Vision Creates Perspective. *Journal of Library Administration*, pp. 55(2), 121-130.

Feldman, R. A. (2004). Jukebox history gets a hit from district court. *Corporate Legal Times*, 14(148), 8-8.

Fife, B. (2015). Disruptive Technologies--Our Time of Transformation. *International Musician*, 113 Issue 7, p4-4.

Fitzpatrick, E. (2001). Labels Resist New Deal. (cover story). *Billboard*, 113(9), 1.

Foster, J. G. (2014). Climbing the Charts: What Radio Airplay Tells Us about the Diffusion of Innovation. *American Journal of Sociology*, 58(3), 491-492.

Franco, F. (2012). Interviews – Learning the Craft of Qualitative Research Interviewing. *European Accounting Review*, 21 (1) 186-189.

Gale. (2006). *Capturing Sound: How Technology Has Changed Music*. Retrieved from Gale Group: http://ic.galegroup.com/ic/bic1/AcademicJournalsDetailsPage/AcademicJournalsDetailsWindow?displayGroupName=Journals&prodId=BIC2&action=e&windowstate=normal&catId=&documentId=GALE%7CA143618095&mode=view&userGroupName=tec_u_online&source=Bookmark&u=tec_u_on

Gaya, H. J., & Smith, E. E. (2016). Developing a Qualitative Single Case Study in the Strategic Management Realm: An Appropriate Research Design? *International Journal of Business Management & Economic Research*, 7(2), 529-538.

Goodwill, S. (2014). *Digital Literacy: Theoretical Framework*. Retrieved from Seattle Goodwill: http://www.seattlegoodwill.org/system/assets/general/JTE/Digital%20Literacy/DL-TheoreticalFramework-1014.pdf

Google. (2015). *Marketing solutions for large businesses*. Retrieved from Google Analytics: http://www.google.com/analytics/

Gough, D., Thomas, J., & Oliver, S. (2012). Clarifying differences between review designs and methods. *Systematic Reviews*. Retrieved from Systematic Reviews.

Group, G. (1998). *Bessie Smith*. Retrieved from Encyclopedia of World Biography: http://ic.galegroup.com/ic/bic1/BiographiesDetailsPage/BiographiesDetailsWindow?disableHighlighting=true&displayGroupName=Biographies&currPage=&scanId=&query=&search_within_results=&p=BIC1&mode=view&catId=GALE%7C00000000MR7B&limiter=&display-query=&displa

Group, G. (1998). *Sergei Vasilievich Rachmaninov*. Retrieved from Encyclopedia of World Biography: http://ic.galegroup.com/ic/bic1/BiographiesDetailsPage/BiographiesDetailsWindow?disableHighlighting=true&displayGroupName=Biographies&currPage=&scanId=&query=&search_within_results=&p=BIC1&mode=view&catId=GALE%7CZZOQAX068476881&limiter=&dis

Group, U. M. (2016). *Universal Music Group*. Santa Monica, CA: MarketLine Company Profile.

Group, W. M. (2016). *Warner Music Group Corp*. New York, NY: Marketline Company Profile.

Gruenwedel, E. (2000, May 1). Net radio daze. *AdWeek: Eastern Edition*, p. 18.

Guardian. (2004, November 20). *Saturday Review: Dispatches: From the archives: Invention of the phonograph, reported in the Manchester Guardian, September 15 1888*. Retrieved from Guardian Newspapers Limited: http://search.proquest.com.proxy.cecybrary.com/docview/246293464?accountid=45927

Gundersen, E. (2005, August 25). Music videos changing places ; Internet options, grassroots efforts are revolutionizing that onetime MTV mainstay. *USA Today*, pp. E-1.

Gutmann, J. (2014). Qualitative research practice: a guide for social science students and researchers (2nd ed.). *International Journal of Market Research*, 56(3), 407-409.

Halker, C. (1993). Music Matters: The Performer and the American Federation of Musicians. *Labor History*, 34(2/3), 389-390.

Hampton-Sosa, W. (2014). Unauthorized Downloading and Purchasing Intention of Digital Culture Products Through Online Streaming Services: The Relevance of Exchange Interface Attributes. *Proceedings for the Northeast Region Decision Sciences Institute (NEDSI)*. , 340-374.

Hannah, S. T., Sumanth, J. J., Lester, P., & Cavarretta, F. (2014, July). Debunking the false dichotomy of leadership idealism and pragmatism: Critical evaluation and support of newer genre leadership theories. *Journal of Organizational Behavior*, pp. 35(5), 598-621.

Hardy, P. (2001). *Frank Walker*. London: Faber & Faber.

Harley, C., Metcalf, L., & Irwin, J. (2014). An Exploratory Study in Community Perspectives of Sustainability Leadership in the Murray Darling Basin. *Journal of Business Ethics*, 124(3) 413-433.

Heer, J. (2001). While Napster enjoyed worldwide popularity soon after its release, it was widely criticized for facilitating copyright infringement. In December of 1999, the Recording Industry Association of America sued Napster, eventually forcing it to shut down. *National Post*, B1.

Hickson, I. M. (2011). Counting to one: The qualitative researcher's 'magic'. *Journal of Occupational & Organizational Psychology*, 84(4), 651-655.

Holland, B. (1994). Biz-related unions back performance right bill. *Bullboard*, 106(19), 5.

Holloway, D. E., & Schaefer, T. (2014). Practitioner Perspectives on Leadership in Small Business. *International Journal of the Academic Business World*, pp. 8(2), 27-36.

Homburg, C., Klarmann, M., Reimann, M., & Schilke, O. (2012, August). What Drives Key Informant Accuracy? *Journal of Marketing Research (JMR)*, pp. 49(4), 594-608.

Hong, S.-H. (2013). Measuring the effect of Napster on recorded music sales: Difference in differences estimates compositional changes. *Journal of Applied Econometrics*, 28(2), 297-324.

Hook, M. (2015, March 18). *Tackling The Digital Skills Gap In The Marketing And Advertising Industries*. Retrieved from Forbes CMO Network: https://www.forbes.com/sites/onmarketing/2015/03/18/tackling-the-digital-skills-gap-in-the-marketing-and-advertising-industries/#69a0614ee422

Hootsuite. (2015). *Enhance Your Social Media and Grow Your Business Today*. Retrieved from Hootsuite: http://signup.hootsuite.com/pro-ent-na-english-r7t/?mkwid=cO9BcqAP_dc&pcrid=7362495645&pkw=hootsuite%20pro&pmt=be&cntry=na-usa&utm_source=bing&utm_medium=cpc&utm_campaign=hootsuite_pro_bing_search_usa_english_branded_alpha

Howell, J. P., Bowen, D. E., Dorfman, P. W., Kerr, S., & Podsakoff, P. M. (1990). Substitutes for Leadership: Effective Alternatives to Ineffective Leadership. *Organizational Dynamics*, pp. 19(1), 20-38.

Hracs, B. J. (2012). A Creative Industry in Transition: The Rise of Digitally Driven Independent Music Production. *Growth & Change*, 43(3), 442-461.

Inslegers, R., Vanheule, S., Meganck, R., Debaere, V., Trenson, E., Desmet, M., & Roelstraete, B. (2012). The Assessment of the Social Cognition and Object Relations Scale on TAT and Interview Data. *Inslegers, Ruth*, 94(4) 372-379.

Iordanoglou, D., & Ioannidis, K. (2014). ESSENTIAL LEADERSHIP SKILLS FOR YOUNG PROFESSIONALS IN TIMES OF CRISIS. *EssentiallLeadership skills for young professionals in times of crisis*, pp. 19, 359-364.

Jarman, K. H. (2015). *Beyond Basic Statistics: Tips, Tricks, and Techniques Every Data Analyst Should Know*. Hoboken, NJ: John Wiley and Sons.

Jones, B. D., Rakes, L., & Landon, K. (2013, October). Malawian secondary students' beliefs about intelligence. *International Journal of Psychology*, pp. 48(5), 785-796.

Juravich, T. (2015). Making music pay: Unfree masters: Recording artists and the politics of work. *New Labor Forum*, 24(3), 104-107.

Kaplan, A. M., & Haenlein, M. (2010). Users of the world, unite! The challenges and opportunities of Social Media. *Business Horizons*, 53(1), 59–68.

Kappelman, L., Jones, M. C., Johnson, V., McClean, E. R., & Boonme, K. (2016, August). Skills for Success at Different Stages of an IT Professional's Career. *Communications of the ACM*, pp. Vol. 59 Issue 8, p64-70.

Katz, B. (2013). *iTunes Music - Mastered for iTunes and the Independent Artist*. Safari Books Online. http://proquestcombo.safaribooksonline.com.proxy.cecybrary.com/book/hardware-and-gadgets/9780415656856/introduction/subhead_4_xhtml?query=(((CD+Baby+Music+Distribution)))#snippet.

Katzenbach, J., Oelschlegel, C., & Thomas, J. (2016, February 15). *10 Principles of Organizational Culture*. Retrieved from Strategy + Business: http://www.strategy-business.com/article/10-Principles-of-Organizational-Culture?gko=71d2f

Kayser, V., Goluchowicz, K., & Bierwisch, A. (2014, June). Test Mining for Technology Roadmapping –The Strategic Value of Information. *International Journal of Innovation Management*, pp. 18(3), 1-23.

Kelly, T. (2005). iTunes set to kill its rivals. *B&T Weekly*, 54(2542), 10.

Kemp, C. (1995). *Music industry management and promotion*. Huntington, UK: Elm Publications.

Keshtiaray, N., & Akbarian, A. (2012). Internet users lived experiences of cultural values (values, norms and verbal symbols) changes in Iran higher education: Ethics and philosophy topics. *Electronic Journal of Information Systems Evaluation*, 15(3), 269-275.

Klenke, K. (2016). *Qualitative Research in the Study of Leadership*. WA, UK: Emerald Group.

Knopper, S. (2011). The Music Biz Bounces Back? *Rolling Stone*, 13-14.

Knopper, S. (2012). Is the CD Era Finally Over. *Rolling Stone*, (1151), 13-14.

Koed, A., & Gay, P. d. (2013). *Doing cultural studies:The story of the sony walkman*. Thousand Oaks, California: Sage .

Kozanczyn, C., Collins, K., & Fernandez, C. V. (2007). Offering Results to Research Subjects: U.S. Institutional Review Board Policy. *Accountability in Research: Policies & Quality Assurance.*, 14(4), 255-267.

Krishnan, R. T., & Jha, S. K. (2011, September). Innovation Strategies in Emerging Markets: What Can We Learn from Indian Market Leaders. *ASCI Journal of Management*, pp. 41(1), 21-45.

Kurtzman, T. (2016). The day big music died. *Journal of Internet Law*, 20(1), 1-11.

Lapan, S. D., Quartaroli, M. T., & Riemer, F. J. (2012). *Qualitative Research: An Introduction to Methods and Designs*. San Francisco: Jossey-Bass.

Lawson, L. (2004). Unmasking Hidden Commercials in Broadcasting: Origins of the Sponsorship Identification Regulations, 1927-1963. *Federal Communications Law Journal*, 329-376.

Leeds, J. (2004, February 4). *Online Song Sales, Though Rising Fast, Are at Most a Hopeful Blip*. Retrieved from Los Angeles Times: http://articles.latimes.com/2004/feb/01/business/fi-online1

Leiter, R. D. (1953). *The Musicians and Petrillo*. New York: Bookman Associates.

Lewis, S. (2014). Positive adaptive leadership and key principles of practice in a time of uncertainty. *AI Practitioner*, 16(1), 20-24.

Lewis, S. (2015). Qualitative Inquiry and Research Design: Choosing Among Five Approaches. *Health Promotion Practice*, 16(4), 473 - 475.

Li, C. (2010). *Open Leadership: How Social Technology Can Transform the Way You Lead*. San Francisco, CA: jossey-Bass.

Liebert, B., Wind, J., & Finley, M. (2015). *Is Your Leadership Style Right for the Digital Age?* Retrieved from Knowledge@Wharton: http://knowledge.wharton.upenn.edu/article/the-right-leadership-style-for-the-digital-age/

Liedtke, M. (2003, April 30). Record labels sue Napster investors: [HOME Edition]. *Daily Breeze*, pp. C3, Retrieved from http://search.proquest.com.proxy.cecybrary.com/docview/338550329?accountid=45847.

Lillegraven, T., & Wilberg, E. (2016). Editor, executive and entrepreneur: Strategic paradoxes in the digital age. *Nordicom review: Nordic research on media & communication*, (37), 115-130.

Lodish, L. M., Morgan, H. L., Archambeau, S., & Babin, J. (2015). *Marketing That Works: How Entrepreneurial Marketing Can Add Sustainable Value to Any Sized Company, Second Edition*. Old Tappan, NJ: Pearson FT Press.

Logan, K. (2013). And now a word from our sponsor: Do consumers perceive advertising on traditional television and online streaming video differently? *Journal of Marketing Communications.*, 19(4), 258-276.

Lunde, A. S. (1948). The American Federation of Musicians and the Recording Ban. *Public Opinion Quarterly. Spring 48*, Vol. 12 Issue 1, p45-56. 12p.

Magoun, A. B. (2000). *Shaping the sound of music: The evolution of the phonograph record, 1877–1950*. Retrieved from ProQuest Central; ProQuest Dissertations & Theses Global:

https://search-proquest-com.proxy.cecybrary.com/docview/304628292/fulltextPDF/99FA1E6F2F6B40DDPQ/1?accountid=26967

Mahembe, B., & Engelbrecht, A. S. (2013). A confirmatory factor analytical study of a servant leadership measure in South Africa. *SAJIP: South African Journal of Industrial Psychology*, pp. 39(2), 1-8.

Majid, R. A., Yassin, S. F., Ishak, N. M., & Rahmat, R. A. (2012). A Study on Graduate and Undergraduate Students' Aspects of Leadership Characteristics. *International Journal of Knowledge, Culture & Change Management*, pp. 11(6), 153-161.

Mancuso, J., & Stuth, K. (2011). What Qualitative Researchers Can Learn from Facebook. *Marketing Research*, 23(2), 32-32.

Manz, C. C. (2015, February). Taking the self-leadership high road: Smooth surface on potholes ahead? *Academy of Management Perspectives*, pp. 29(1), 132-151.

Marques, J. (2013). Understanding the Strength of Gentleness: Soft-Skilled Leadership on the Rise. *Journal of Business Ethics*, Vol. 116 Issue 1, p163-171.

Marshall, C., & Rossman, G. B. (2015). Designing Qualitative Research, Sixth Edition. *Canadian Journal of Sociology*, 40(3), 399-401.

Matthew, C. T., Buontempo, G., & Block, C. J. (2013, March). Relational approach to work: conceptual definition and scale development. *Journal of Applied Social Psychology*, pp. 43(3), 507-514.

Maxwell, J. A. (2013). *Qualitative Research Design: An Interactive Approach (3rd Ed.).* Thousand Oaks, California: Sage.

Mayer, I. (2014, May). The research and evaluation of serious games: Toward a comprehensive methodology. *British Journal of Educational Technology.*, pp. 45(3), 502-527.

Meera, M. (2010). Library and Information Professionals (LIPs) in the Present Digital age: Challenges of the new Skills. *Proceedings of the International Conference on Information Management & Evaluation*, 228-236.

Menell, P. S. (2012). Infringement Conflation. *Stanford Law Review*, 1551-1582.

Meneses, J. P. (2012). About Pandora and other streaming music services: the new active consumer on radio. *Observatorio*, 6(1), 235-257.

Merriam, S. B., & Tisdell, E. J. (2016). *Qualitative Research: A Guide to Design and Implementation.* San Francisco: Jossey-Bass.

Mertens, D. M. (2015). *Research and Evaluation in Education and Psychology: Integrating Diversity ...* Thousand Oaks, California: Sage.

Messing, K., Caroly, S., Ahlgren, C., & Gillander Gådin, K. (2011). Struggle for time to teach: Teachers' experiences of their work situation. *Work*, 40, 111-118.

Mikesell, L., Bromley, E., & Khodyakov, D. (n.d.). Ethical Community-Engaged Research: A Literature Review. *American Journal of Public Health*, pp. 103(12), e7-e14.

Millage, A. (2015, February). Value Through leadership. *Internal Auditor*, pp. 72, 7.

Milliken, F. J., Morrison, E. W., & Hewlin, P. F. (2003). An Exploratory Study of Employee Silence: Issues that Employees Don't Communicate Upward and Why. *Journal of Management Studies.*, 40(6), 1453-1476.

Mirocha, J., Bents, R., LaBrosse, M., & Rietow, K. (2013). Strategies for Developing Leaders in Small to Medium Sized Firms: An Analysis of Best Practices in the Most Successful Firms. *Organization Development Journal*, 31(3), 23-38.

Mojtahed, R., Nunes, M. B., Martins, J. T., & Peng, A. (2014). Equipping the Constructivist Researcher: The Combined use of Semi-Structured Interviews and Decision-Making maps. *Electronic Journal of Business Research Methods*, pp. 12(2) 87-95.

Money, A. (2016). *Emile Berliner - The History of the Gramophone.* Retrieved from About Money: http://inventors.about.com/od/gstartinventions/a/gramophone.htm

Monkeyshines. (2001). Sergei Rachmaninoff. *Monkeyshines on Music & Great Musicians*, 88.

Moreau, F. (2013). The Disruptive Nature of Digitization: The Case of the Recorded Music Industry. *International Journal of Arts Management*, pp. 15(2), 18-31.

Morris, A. (2013). Playing for Change: Music and Musicians in the Service of Social Movements. *American Journal of Sociology*, 73, 392-394.

Morris, J. W., & Powers, D. (2015). Control, curation and musical experience in streaming music services. *Creative Industries Journal*, 8(2), 106-122.

Mossig, I. (2008). Global Networks of the Motion Picture Industry in Los Angeles/Hollywood using the Example of their Connections to the German Market. *European Planning Studies*, 16(1), 43-59.

Moulton, D. (2001, April 6). When eight-tracks ruled the road: Now in bargain bins, eight-tracks were once the only music made for cars: [Toronto Edition]. *National Post*, p. F4.

Moustakas, C. (1994). *Phenomenological Research Methods.* Thousand Oaks, CA: Sage.

Musolino, C., Warin, M., Wade, T., & Gilchrist, P. (2016, December 16). Developing shared understandings of recovery and care: a qualitative study of women with eating disorders who resist therapeutic care. *Journal of Eating Disorders*, pp. 4, 1-10.

Nelson, J. (2010, November 22). Sony Walkman (1979-2010). *Canadian Business*, pp. 83(19), 27.

Newspapers, M. (1996). New MTV service leads next generation analysts predict number of home cable channels could soar to 160 over decade. *Wisconsin State Journal*, 5B. Retrieved from http://search.proquest.com.proxy.cecybrary.com/docview/390692880?accountid=45927.

Nielsen Business Media, I. (1971, April). Frank Walker and Loews Inc. *Billboard*, (83), 14.

Northouse, P. G. (2013). Skills Approach. In P. G. Northouse, *Leadership Theory and Practice. Sixth Edition* (p. 43). Thousand Oaks: SAGE.

Norton, J. A., & Bass, F. M. (2012). Evolution of technological generations: The law of capture. *Sloan Management Review*, 33(2), 66.

Orzan, G., Burghelea, I., Stupu, L.-D., & Boboc, A.-L. (2016). The impact of social media conversations on brand image of cloud computing. *Annals of the University of Oradea, Economic Science Series*, 25(1), 1002-1010.

Owsinski, B. (2016). Music 4.1: A Survival Guide for Making Music in the Internet Age. *Protoview*, 3(33).

Padgett, D. (2017). *Qualitative Methods in Social Work Research*. Thousand Oaks California: Sage.

Panteras, G., Wise, S., Lu, X., Croitoru, A., Crooks, A., & Stefanidis, A. (2015, October). Triangulating Social Multimedia Content for Event Localization using Flickr and Twitter. *Transactions in GIS*, pp. 19(5), 694-715.

Parr-Scanlin, D. (2010, June). Chopin: 21 Mazurkas. *Entertainment Review*, pp. 2(3), 65.

Patel, T., & Hamlin, R. G. (2012, November). Deducing a taxonomy of perceived managerial and leadership effectiveness: a comparative study of effective and ineffective managerial behaviour across three EU countries. *Human Resource Development International*, pp. 15(5), 571-587.

Peinado, J., & Graeml, A. R. (2016). Mapping of Themes Pertaining to Operations Management: a Refined Analysis Based on the Perceptions of Researchers, Lecturers and Practitioners. *Brazilian Business Review (English Edition)*, pp. 13(2), 82-104.

Peoples, G. (2015, November 5). *Pandora and Sony/ATV Reach Multi-Year Agreement*. Retrieved from Billboard.com: http://www.billboard.com/articles/business/6753769/pandora-sony-atv-multi-year-licensing-agreement

Peppard, J., & Ward, J. (2016). *The Strategic Management of Information Systems: Building a Digital Strategy*. United Kingdom: Wiley: John Wiley & Sons.

Phelps, K. C. (2014). 'So Much Technology, So Little Talent'? Skills for Harnessing Technology for Leadership Outcomes. *Journal of Leadership Studies*. , 8(2), 51-56.

Phillips, P., Ray, R., & Phillips, J. J. (2016). How to Capture the Business Value of Leadership Development. *People & Strategy*, pp. Vol. 39, p46-51.

Pikas, B., Pikas, A., & Lymburner, C. (2011). The Future of the Music Industry. *Journal of Marketing Development & Competitiveness*, 5(3), 139-149.

Pinta, E. R. (2008). The First RCA Victor Recording of 1948: Petrillo, Truman and the AFM Recording Ban of 1948. *ARSC Journal*, 39(2), 284-291.

Plummer, M. (2014, July 7). *Apple Pro Training Series: GarageBand - Lesson 2. Working with Tracks*. Retrieved from Safari:

http://proquestcombo.safaribooksonline.com.proxy.cecybrary.com/book/audio/9780133901054/lesson-2dot-working-with-tracks/ch02_html?query=(((Tape+Recorders+Revolutionize+music+industry)))#snippet

Pojasek, R. B. (2012). Checking and Reviewing Sustainability Progress. *Environmental Quality Management*, pp. 22(2), 83-91.

Pontis, S., & Blandford, A. (2015). Understanding 'influence:' an exploratory study of academics' processes of knowledge construction through iterative and interactive information seeking. *Journal of the Association for Information Science & Technology*, 66(8), 1576-1593.

Posner, B. Z. (2016, December). Investigating the Reliability and Validity of the Leadership Practices Inventory. *Administrative Sciences*, pp. 6(4), 1-23.

Pozner, B. (2016). Investigating the Reliability and Validity of the Leadership Practices Inventory®. *Administrative Sciences*, 6(4), 1-23.

Pras, A., Guastavino, C., & Lavoie, M. (2013, March). The impact of technological advances on recording studio practices. *Journal of the American Society for Information Science & Technology*, pp. 64(3), 612-626.

Prasad, A., Green, P., & Heales, J. (2013). On Governing Collaborative Information Technology (IT): A Relational Perspective. *Journal of Information Systems*, pp. 27(1), 237-259.

Prieto, B. (2013, June). Establishing and Building Leadership Skills. *Leadership & Management in Engineering.*, pp. 13(3), 209-211.

Productions, S. (2017). *ICT*. Retrieved from Home : Internet Terms : ICT Definition: https://techterms.com/definition/ict

Quaquebeke, N., & Eckloff, T. (2010, February). Defining Respectful Leadership: What It Is, How It Can Be Measured, and Another Glimpse at What It Is Related to. *Journal of Business Ethics*, pp. 91(3), 343-358.

Ramsey, M., & Barkhuizen, N. (2011). Organisational design elements and competencies for optimising the expertise of knowledge workers in a shared services centre. *South African Journal of Human Resource Management*, 9(1), 158-172.

Rennhoff, A. D. (2010). The consequences of "consideration payments": Lessons from radio payola. *Review of Industrial Organization.*, 36(2), 133-147.

Research, N. C. (2012). *The Belmont Report: Ethical Principles and Guidelines for the Protection of Human Subjects of Research, Vol. 1* . Washington D.C.: DHEW.

Review, H. L. (1999). The criminalization of copyright infringement in the digital era. *Harvard Law Review*, 112(7), 1705.

Riggs, T. (2015). *Gale Encyclopedia of U.S. Economic History (2nd ed.)*. Farmington Hills, MI: Gale.

Ritchie, J., Lewis, J., Nicholls, McNaughton, C., & Ormston, R. (2014). *Qualitative Research Practice: A Guide for Social Science Students and Researchers.* Thousand Oaks, California: Sage.

Robb, S. L., Clair, A. A., Watanabe, M., Monahan, P. O., Azzouz, F., Stouffer, J. W., . . . Wh, C. (2007). Randomized controlled trial of the active music engagement (AME) intervention on children with cancer. *Psycho-Oncology*, 17(7), 699-708.

Robertson, K., McNeill, L., Green, J., & Roberts, C. (2012). Illegal Downloading, Ethical Concern, and Illegal Behavior. *Journal of Business Ethics*, 108(2), 215-227.

Robinson, O. C. (2014). Sampling in Interview-Based Qualitative Research: A Theoretical and Practical Guide. *Qualitative Research in Psychology*, 11(1), 25-41.

Rogers, W., & Meek Lange, M. (2013, December). Rethinking the Vulnerability of Minority Populations in Research. *American Journal of Public Health*, pp. 103(12), 2141-2146.

Rossman, G. (2012). *Climbing the Charts: What Radio Airplay Tells Us about the Diffusion of Innovation.* Princeton, New Jersey: Princeton University Press.

Rubin, E. N. (2013). Assessing your leadership style to achieve organizational objectives. *Global Business & Organizational Excellence*, 32(6), 55-66.

Rubin, H., & Rubin, I. (2012). *Qualitative Interviewing: The Art of Hearing Data - Third Edition.* Thousand Oaks, CA: SAGE.

Russ-Mohl, S., Wilczek, B., & Nienstedt, H.-W. (2013). *Journalism and Media Convergence.* Berlin : De Gruyter.

Sanderlin-Nykamp, D. J. (2011). *An exploratory study of executive leadership in social work.* Ann Arbor: DAI-A 72/08, Dissertation Abstracts International.

Sarma, G. S. (2015). The use of online forums and chatrooms to enhance student participation: An innovative approach. *Proceedings for the Northeast Region Decision Sciences Institute (NEDSI)*, 1-11.

Schatz, E. (2012, July). Rationale and procedures for nesting semi-structured interviews in surveys or censuses. *Population Studies*, pp. 66(2), 183-195.

Schreier, M. (2012). *Qualitative Content Analysis in Practice.* Thousand Oaks, California: Sage.

Scollon, S., Bergstrom, K., Kerstein, R. A., Tao Wang, S. G., Ramamurthy, U., Gibbs, R. A., . . . Parsons, D. W. (2014). Obtaining informed consent for clinical tumor and germline exome sequencing of newly diagnosed childhood cancer patients. *Genome Medicine*, 6(9), 69.

Seff, J. (2001). Apple's Music Man. *Macworld*, 18(3), 39. Retrieved from TidBITS: https://leanpub.com/p/takecontrol

Seidensticker, B. (2006). Part 1: The Way We See Technology Incorrectly. In B. Seidensticker, *Future Hype: The Myths of Technology Change* (p. 116). San Francisco: Berrett-Koehler Publishers.

Shapero, D. (2015). The Impact of Technology on Music Stars' Cultural Influence. *Elon Journal of Undergraduate research in communications*, 6(1), 1-2.

Sheehan, B., Tsao, J., & Pokrywcznski, J. (2012). Stop the music! *Journal of Advertising Research*, 52(3), 309-321.

Sinek, S. (2009). *Start with Why: How Great Leaders Inspire Everyone to Take Action*. New York, New York: Penguin Group.

Singh, H. P., & Tarray, T. A. (2015). On the Use of Randomization Device for Estimating the Proportion and Truthful Reporting of a Qualitative Sensitive Attribute. *Pakistan Journal of Statistics & Operation Research*, pp. Vol. 11 Issue 1, p29-40.

Sloane, G. (2014). Sloane, Garett. *Adweek*, 55(26), 14.

Smith, N., Wollan, R., & Zhou, C. (2011). *The Social Meida Management Handbook: Everything You Need To Know To Get Social Media Working In Your Business*. Hoboken, New Jersey: Wiley.

Software, I.-L. (2016). *What About*. Retrieved from FL Studio 12: https://www.image-line.com/flstudio/

Spotts, H. E. (2010). We'd rather fight than switch: Music industry in a time of change. *Journal of the International Academy for Case Studies*, 16(5), 33-46.

Stergiou-Kita, M., Grigorovich, V., Tseung, E., Milosevic, D., Hebert, S., & Phan, J. J. (2014). Qualitative meta-synthesis of survivors' work experiences and the development of strategies to facilitate return to work. *Journal of Cancer Survivorship*, 657–670.

Sterne, J. (2012). *MP3: The Meaning of A Format*. Durham, North Carolina: Duke University Press.

Stocks, J. (2010). Ethics and the Responsible Conduct of Research. *Council on Undergraduate Research Quarterly*, 30(3), 10.

Stross, R. (2010, July 5). The Incredible Talking Machine. *Time Magazine*, pp. 176(1), 48-49.

SXSW. (2017, March 6). *Music Festival*. Retrieved from South by Southwest (SXSW): https://www.sxsw.com/festivals/music/

Tait, A. R., & Voepel-Lewis, T. (2015). Digital Multimedia: A New Approach for Informed Consent? *JAMA. American Medical Association*, 463-464.

Tanaka, K. (2003). On tape-cut editing with a fixed head type PCM tape recorder. *IEEE Transactions on Acoustics, Speech, and Signal Processing*, 27(6) 739 - 745. Retrieved from http://ieeexplore.ieee.org/abstract/document/1163299/?reload=true

Tannenbaum, R., & Marks, C. (2011). *I Want My MTV: The Uncensored Story of the Music Video Revolution*. New York, New York: Penguin Group.

Tattersall, P. (2012). The great race: Investment managers apply new technologies to get ahead. *Journal of Securities Operations & Custody*, pp. 4(4), 333-345.

Taylor, S. J., Bogdan, R., & DeVault, M. (2016). *Introduction to Qualitative Research Methods: A Guidebook and Resource*. Hoboken, New Jersey: John Wiley & Sons.

Titko, J., & Lace, N. (2011). Triangulation Research Design for Studying of the Concept of Bank Value. *Economics & Management*, 16, 974-980.

Tschmuck, P. (2010). *Creativity and Innovation in the Music Industry*. Dordrecht, The Netherlands: Springer.

Tucker, S. (2011, December). *10 Best Social Media Sites for Small Business Owners*. Retrieved from Get Susan Marketing: http://get-susan.com/services/10-best-social-media-sites-for-small-business-owners/

Turner, J. (2012). The Planning of Guaranteed Targeted Display Advertising. *Operations Research*, 60(1), 18-33.

Tyldum, G. (2012). Ethics or access? Balancing informed consent against the application of institutional, economic or emotional pressures in recruiting respondents for research. *International Journal of Social Research Methodology*, 15(3), 199-210.

UCSB. (2017). *Columbia Phonograph Co. Cylinders*. Retrieved from UCSB Cylinder Audio Archive: http://cylinders.library.ucsb.edu/history-columbia.php

University, B. (2016). *Institutional Review Board (IRB):What is the IRB*. Retrieved from HRPP/IRB: https://www.brown.edu/research/conducting-research-brown/research-compliance-irb-iacuc-coi-export-control/hrppirb-home-page

University, C. (2007-2008). *Dissertation Guides Workbook*. Retrieved from Capella.edu: http://www.capella.edu/interactivemedia/Colloquia/docs/DissertationGuidesWorkbook-T3.pdf

Unlimited, J. (2013). *Wurlitzer, 150 years in as many words*. Retrieved from Jukeboxes Unlimited: http://www.jukebox-uk.biz/wurlitzer-150-years

Vagle, M. D. (2016). *Crafting Phenomenological Research*. New York, New York: Routledge.

Venters, J. W., Green, M. T., & Lopez, D. M. (2012). Social media: A leadership challenge. *Business Studies Journal*, 4, 85-93.

Vignehsa, K. (2015). Genealogical Ethnography: Process Thinking to Study the 'Inside' of Projects. *Project Management Journal*, 46(2), 60-72.

Wang, P., Chen, X., Gong, J., & Jacques-Tiura, A. (2014, November). Reliability and Validity of the Personal Social Capital Scale 16 and Personal Social Capital Scale 8: Two Short Instruments for Survey Studies. *Social Indicators Research*, pp. 119(2), 1133-1148.

Week, N. (2008). Fierce festive battle ahead as majors fight over artist albums crown. *News Week*, (51), 2-3.

Weijters, B., Goedertier, F., & Verstreken, S. (2014, November). Online Music Consumption in Today's Technological Context: Putting the Influence of Ethics in Perspective. *Journal of Business Ethics*, pp. 124, 537-550.

Weitzl, W. (2016). Measuring Electronic Word-of-Mouth Effectiveness. In W. Weitzl, *Conceptualization of the Construct, Research Questions and Hypotheses* (pp. pp 95-162). Austria: Gabler Verlag.

Westegren, T. (2009). Tailor your product to 1 million customers. *Financial Executive*, 25(8), 38-38.

White, T. (1994, November). His master's voice: A matter of trust. *Billboard Magazine*, pp. 106(44), 53.

Wijnhoven, F., & Brinkhuis, M. (2015, April). Internet information triangulation: Design theory and prototype evaluation. *Journal of the Association for Information Science & Technology*, pp. 66(4), 684-701.

Winn, B. (2013). Learning to lead with cultural intelligence (CQ): When do global leaders learn best? *People & Strategy*, pp. 36(3), 10-13.

Wolgemuth, J. R. (2014, October). Analyzing for critical resistance in narrative research. *Qualitative Research*, pp. 14(5), 586-602.

Wood, R. L. (2015). 10/9 - Integral Leadership for a Regenerative, Inclusive Economy. *Integral Leadership Review.*, pp. 242-249.

Wright, G. (2015). An empirical examination of the relationship between nonresponse rate and nonresponse bias. *Statistical Journal of the IAOS*, 31(2), 305-315.

Wueller, J. R. (2013). Mergers of Majors: Applying the failing firm doctrine in the recorded music industry. *Brooklyn Journal of Corporate, Financial & Commercial Law*, pp. 7(2), 589-612.

Xu, X. M., & Storr, G. B. (2012). Learning the Concept of Researcher as Instrument in Qualitative Research. *The Qualitative Report*, 1-18.

Yang, S. (2013, January). Surviving as a qualitative researcher in a quantitative world: a personal reflection. *International Journal of Social Research Methodology*, pp. 16(1), 81-85.

Yin, R. K. (2016). *Qualitative Research from Start to Finish, Second Edition.* New York: Gilford Press.

Zak, A. J. (2003). *Capturing Sound: How Technology Has Changed Music.* Retrieved from http://ic.galegroup.com/ic/bic1/AcademicJournalsDetailsPage/AcademicJournalsDetails Window?displayGroupName=Journals&prodId=BIC2&action=e&windowstate=normal &catId=&documentId=GALE%7CA143618095&mode=view&userGroupName=tec_u_o nline&source=Bookmark&u=tec_u_on

MY SUCCESS STEPS AND JOURNAL

MY SUCCESS STEPS AND JOURNAL

DATE

My Success Steps and Journal

DATE

www.ingramcontent.com/pod-product-compliance
Lightning Source LLC
Chambersburg PA
CBHW020436220526
45464CB00002B/733